Who's Guarding the Gates? Study Guide

by
Nancy L Robinson

Copyright © 2012 by Nancy L Robinson

Who's Guarding the Gates? Study Guide
by Nancy L Robinson

Printed in the United States of America

ISBN 9781624191862

All rights reserved solely by the author. The author guarantees all contents are original and do not infringe upon the legal rights of any other person or work. No part of this book may be reproduced in any form without the permission of the author. The views expressed in this book are not necessarily those of the publisher.

Unless otherwise indicated, Bible quotations are taken from The Holy Bible, NIV®. Copyright © 1973, 1978, 1984, by International Bible Society. Used by permission of Zondervan Publishing House; The "NIV" and "New International Version" trademarks are registered in the United States Patent and Trademark Office by International Bible Society. Use of either trademark requires the permission of International Bible Society; The New American Standard Bible (NASB). Copyright © 1960, 1962, 1963, 1968, 1971, 1972, 1973, 1975, 1977, 1995 by The Lockman Foundation; The Holy Bible, New Living Translation (NLT). Copyright © 1996, 2004, 2007. Used by permission of Tyndale House Publishers, Inc.; The Amplified Bible (AMP). Copyright © 1954, 1958, 1964, 1987 by The Lockman Foundation; The Holy Bible, King James Version, Cambridge Edition (KJV); The Holy Bible, New King James Version (NKJV). Copyright © 1979, 1980, 1982 by Thomas Nelson, Inc.; and The Holy Bible, English Standard Version (ESV). Copyright © 2001 by Crossway Bibles. Used by permission.

www.xulonpress.com

Contents

Part One.......15

Defining the Gates

1. The Significance of the Gates.......17

Part Two.......25

The Ear Gates

2. Unclogging the Gates...27
3. When Reason is Asleep.......32

Part Three....37

The Eye Gates

4. Do You Wish to See?......39
5. A Holy Gaze......47

6. A Faulty Lamp.......53

Part Four......59

The Heart Gate

7. Bring Him the Broken Pieces......61
8. A Holy House......67
9. Let's Play Dress-Up......72
10. Good Tree—Good Fruit. Bad Tree—Bad Fruit......78
11. Thy Will Be Done......83

Part Five......89

The Mouth Gate

12. The Words We Speak......91
13. Bent By A Word......97
14. Choose Your Battles....103
15. Abiding in Jesus—The Discipline Of Waiting...108
16. Are You Ready To Rumble?......115

Part Six......121

The Mind Gate

17. Which Way Did I Go?....123
18. A Candidate For Change......132

Contents

19. My Minds' Made Up......139
20. Looking Back......146
21. Delivered From Shame.....152
22. Where Are You Headed? (Dealing with the Wall)....159

Answer Key......169

How to Use This Study Guide

This study guide is designed as a companion to *Who's Guarding the Gates?* by Nancy L. Robinson. As you work through the exercises, questions, and sections written for personal reflection and meditation, you will be challenged in your walk with Jesus Christ, and with others. This study guide can be used for individual, personal spiritual growth as well as for studies in both small and large group settings.

Each chapter of the study guide contains five sections:

Chapter Theme: This provides a brief synopsis of the contents of the entire chapter at a quick glance.

Questions for Discussion: The questions are provided both to challenge each individual in the area of personal growth, as well as to assist in facilitating group discussions. The questions can be asked at any time during the lesson.

Conclusion: This is given to help students understand the overall intent of the chapter.

Applying God's Principles in Our Daily Living (Points to Ponder): Questions and points for reflection and meditation in this section are designed to help the students grow in significant ways in their daily walk with God, and with others. The purpose is to give students real-life opportunities to walk out and to apply what they have learned from each chapter, in practical ways.

Commit to Prayer: Each chapter ends with a heartfelt prayer, petitioning the Father's guidance and graces as students come to deeper levels of insight concerning the importance of guarding the gates to the kingdom of God that exists within them.

The final section of the study guide contains an answer key for your convenience. By the time you have concluded the lessons in this book, it is our fervent prayer that you will discover your own personal walk with God to be significantly stronger than before. You will have gained valuable insight into the importance of guarding your gates. You will be more aware of the strategies of the Enemy against your life to steal what rightfully belongs to you. You will be empowered to hold onto and take back your God-given authority at every gate.

Introduction

When I set out to write about the gates to the kingdom of God that exists within us, some fifteen years ago, it was really nothing more than a monthly newsletter I was writing for my local church. However, as I continued to write and to study about them, I could clearly see that the message concerning the significance of these gates was one that would be a source of great blessing to the kingdom of God on a larger scale.

The Holy Spirit began to give me insight into the significance of the old gates that were erected back in the Bible days. These ancient gates signified authority, safety, prosperity, death and life, amongst other things. Those living back in the Bible days clearly understood the significance of the gates, and many of them would, and did, in fact, manipulate, swindle, lie and kill to gain the seats of authority positioned at the gates to the city's entrances.

According to the gospel of Luke, chapter 17, there is a kingdom of God that exists within each of us. That kingdom also has gates –

our eyes, our ears, our mouths, our hearts and our minds. So many of us today do not realize how important these gates are to our destinies; therefore, in ignorance, we have failed to carefully guard them. Our shrewd Adversary is fully aware of the significance of these gates, and employs new strategies each day to take possession of them through the things that we fix our eyes upon; the words that we speak; the things we listen to; the thoughts in our heads, and the emotions that we harbor in our hearts.

In the years that it took me to complete the book, ***Who's Guarding the Gates?*** I have experienced my own failures in guarding my gates, but I have also had many victories as I learned vital lessons along the way. Some of the failures and victories, I share in the book.

Now, more than ever, we must be ready, willing, and able to effectively stand guard at all of our gates to maintain the authority that God has given to us. This is vital as we see the foundations of righteousness being leveled all around us. We must teach our children and our grandchildren how to guard their gates, and how to hold onto their godly inheritances. The book, ***Who's Guarding the Gates?*** and its companion study guide have been prayerfully written and designed to help you do just that.

God is raising up an army of powerful warriors, men, women and children who are fully equipped to impact His kingdom for His glory. It is my prayer that after you have completed both the book and the study guide you will be one of the many empowered by the

Introduction

Holy Spirit to shake up the kingdom of darkness, and bring glory to God as you regain possession of everything that is rightfully yours.

– Nancy L. Robinson

Part One

Defining the Gates

Chapter 1

The Significance of the Gates

"...and your descendants shall possess the gate of their enemies.
In your seed all the nations of the earth shall be blessed,
because you have obeyed My voice."
Genesis 22:15-18 (NKJV)

Chapter Theme

- The promise from God to Abraham found in Genesis 22:15-18 is indeed powerful, but as with all of the promises from God, there is the contingency of obedience. Certain conditions must be met before the promise can be fulfilled. The Israelites were God's chosen people, set apart to be an example in obedience, righteousness, and holiness to the rest of the world. Abraham displayed unusual obedience when he took his only son to the region of Moriah to offer him up to the Lord as a burnt sacrifice at the commandment of God. His unusual obedience secured the promise of Genesis 22:15-18 for us, for our children, and for our children's children, but for us to maintain that promise, we too must be committed to a radical obedience to the Lord.

Our disobedience to the voice of the Lord has left us weak and exposed to the Enemy of our souls. He has seized an opportunity to prevail upon us in our unguarded state and to steal, not only our stuff, but our very souls. Thanks be unto our God, for He is a Mighty Warrior, our Redeemer and the Lover of our souls. He has not deserted us, but has given us a strategy, to rebuild our gates, and to possess our Enemy's gates in the process.

The Significance of the Gates

The Significance of the Gates

Questions for Discussion

1. According to Genesis 22, what did God ask Abraham to do?

2. How did Abraham respond?

3. As a result of his obedience, what was the promise from God to Abraham?

4. What does it mean to "possess," by the Hebrew definition?

5. What is the dictionary definition of a "gate"?

(noun) _____ _____ or a _____.
(verb) _____ _____ _____ or a _____.

6. From a spiritual standpoint, how significant is a gate?

7. The Word of God exposes Satan as a _____ and a, _____ whose purpose is to _____, _____ and _____ . (Cite the scripture and verse).

Who's Guarding the Gates? Study Guide

8. What does Jesus say that He is?

9. What has been the result of our failure to guard our gates?

10. What has the Old Testament revealed to us about the significance of the gates?

11. List the five functions of the gates, and cite the scripture and verse:

   a. _____ .
   b. _____ .
   c. _____ .
   d. _____ .
   e. _____ .

12. List the six representative (figurative) functions of the gates:

   a. _____ .
   b. _____ .
   c. _____ .
   d. _____ .
   e. _____ .
   f. _____ .

The Significance of the Gates

13. Describe the level of durability and functionality of the following gates:
    a. Gates of wood (Neh. 1:3):
    b. Gates of bronze (Ps. 107:10-19):
    c. Gates of iron (Acts 12:10; Isa. 45:1-3):
    d. Gates of precious stones (Rev. 21:12):

14. What important character trait did Moses possess that made him useful to God to lead the children of Israel to dispossess hostile nations and to regain possession of their gates?

15. What caused the anger of God to burn against the Israelites?

16. How does the Devil keep us content in the land of our captivity?

17. What does 1 Peter 2:9 say about us?

18. Describe how a rodent is caught in a trap and how this parallels our own inability to resist the Enemy's snares?

19. What are the indicators that we are operating in radical disobedience to God?

20. In your own words, briefly explain 1 Peter 2:8.

21. What are the five gates to the kingdom of God that is within us?

    a. _____

    b. _____

    c. _____

    d. _____

    e. _____

22. How difficult has God made it for us to obey His commands?

23. What is the first building material that we need in the reconstruction of our gates?

Conclusion

The promise of Genesis 22:15-18 was for Abraham and his descendants, which would include us. God requires our obedience to His voice and to His commandments. If we are to dispossess the gate of our enemies and regain possession of our own gates, we must humble our hearts and submit our lives to the control of the Holy Spirit. God is intimately concerned about every aspect and detail of our lives in the same way as any good, godly parent is concerned about everything that concerns their child's well being, except God's care for us reaches higher and deeper levels than our own (See Ps. 139).

We must be willing to allow Him to control every aspect and detail of our lives. This control starts at the gates—the eye gates, the ear gates, the heart gate, the mouth gate, and the mind gate. We can walk in abundance, experience a level of intimacy with God, and exercise power over our Adversary we have not previously known once the gates to the kingdom of God within us have been regained and rebuilt.

Applying God's Principles in Our Daily Living

Points to Ponder

- If you could rate your willingness to obey the voice of the Lord in your daily life, what kind of score would you give yourself on a scale of one to ten, ten being the highest? Understanding how the obedience of Abraham has resulted in blessings for us, even today, what things can you do to improve upon your willingness to obey God even in the hard places?
- Have you ever been tested by God in the way that Abraham was tested in Genesis 22? If so, how did you respond? What specific scripture(s) would you use today to help you more readily obey God's voice?

- Do you feel that you have allowed Satan to rob you through your own failure to guard your gates? How? In what ways would you be able to prevent him from robbing you in that same way today, knowing what you now know about the importance of guarding your gates?
- Can you think of a time when you may have considered the price for freedom from bondage to have been too high a price to pay? What did you have to do to finally break free from behind the Enemy's prison gates?

Commit to Prayer

- In Deuteronomy 30:11-14, we are told that the Word of God residing in our hearts and proceeding from our mouths enables us to walk in obedience to God's commandments. As you go before God in prayer, confess those areas of disobedience and compromise in your own life. Ask Him to help you take hold of the grace that He has made available to you for you to obey His instructions and break free from Satan's traps.

Part Two

The Ear Gates

Chapter 2

<u>Unclogging the Gates</u>

To hear, one must be silent. ~ Ursula Le Guin

Chapter Theme

- Simply put, faith comes by hearing. . .we will have faith for whatever it is that we incline our ears to hear, good or bad. There is good faith, and there is bad faith. God wants us to have faith to walk in what He has decreed for us. We must be very careful what we bend down to listen to. The words that we take into our ear gates can define our destiny.

Unclogging the Gates

Questions for Discussion

1. What does Romans 10:17 mean to you?

2. What does Hebrews 11:6 mean to you?

3. What does Romans 14:23 mean to you?

4. What does Hebrews 10:38 mean to you?

5. Circle one: True or False

   Relinquishing the full authority of our ear gates to Satan can happen overnight.

6. What happens each time you listen to someone tell you something about yourself that is contrary to what God says about you?

7. Secular music involves _____ .

8. Briefly explain the dark path of fantasy.

9. When we begin to give ear to the Enemy, it is a sure sign that our hearts are _____ .

Unclogging the Gates

10. What is the most common way that people give up power?

11. What is the significance of Matthew 16:19 to us as believers?

12. Whoever has possession of the keys is the one who _____ _____ _____.

13. What does it mean to "guard"?

14. When we are careless with our authority, we grant our Adversary the license to _____.

15. Men are largely seduced by what enters their _____ _____. Women are largely seduced by what enters their _____ _____.

16. If we are not tuned in to the Holy Spirit's voice, we may think that we are discerning the voice of God, when all the while. _____.

17. A famous Latin proverb says, "_____."

Conclusion

Jesus came that we, His children, might have the abundant life, but Satan, our Adversary, fights to rob us of the riches of our inheritance. He sits at the entrance to our ear gates and waits for opportunities to shout out perversities and lies. While we are distracted and thrown off course by his lies, he creeps in and steals the truths that we have left unguarded. Deeper and deeper he plunges his lies down into our ear gates until hearing the voice of the Lover of our souls is nearly, if not completely, impossible. We must be careful of what we listen to.

Not every voice speaks to edify. Not every voice is speaking truth. Not every voice is speaking to liberate. We recognize the voice of the Good Shepherd by reading and meditating on His Word. His Word is Truth. When we are careful to guard the truths that Jesus speaks to us, then we will be equipped to discern the lies of Satan and quickly turn back his lies at the gate before they have the chance to enter.

Applying God's Principles in Our Daily Living

Points to Ponder

- Have the kinds of things that you have been listening to made you stronger or weaker spiritually? Consider your spiritual diet over the next seven days. Make an unusual spiritual sacrifice by feeding your spirit only worship music, and reading only God's Word (no entertainment magazines, no television). See how much stronger you will feel at the end of the seven-day period. Be prepared to discuss it.

- Can you think of a time when you believed a lie about yourself that Satan planted in your ear gates? What were the results of that lie? What can you do as a safeguard against this type of demonic attack?

Commit to Prayer

- Jesus said that our faith comes by hearing God's Word (Rom. 10:17). If we will be honest with God, we might admit that we have allowed our ear gates to be violated by Satan, making it hard for us to discern the voice of our Shepherd. The inability to hear and be led by our Lord makes it easier for us to wander away from His side, and to be led and held captive by our Enemy. Take some time to confess this to the Lord, and ask for His help in recapturing the gates to your ears so that you are able to hear Him clearly, and get back on the right path for your life.
- Take some time to thank Him for always having His arms open wide to receive you back.

Chapter 3

When Reason is Asleep

Man is born free, but is everywhere in chains!
~ Social Contract (Jean-Jacques Rousseau – 1762)

Chapter Theme

- In the perfect timing of God, He makes all things beautiful. God is never late, and He never forgets that we are waiting on Him and for Him. Every believer will, at some point in their pilgrimage, come to the place along their journey where they will look around and be convinced that they have been walking all alone for quite some time. It will appear as though the Shepherd has abandoned us to our own devices. It is at this juncture of the journey that we begin to listen to demons whisper in our ear gates, "God has abandoned you during the roughest part of your pilgrimage. He has left you to figure out the rest of the way on your own." The thirstiness of our souls will have us agreeing with the Enemy and resorting to crafty methods to attain our desired end. A stint in the desert can make us forget the truths about the character of God. We will reason that He has forgotten to be faithful.

Who's Guarding the Gates? Study Guide

When Reason is Asleep

Questions for Discussion

1. Complete the following verse of scripture: "Then after desire has _____, it gives _____ to _____; and _____, when it is full-grown, gives _____ to _____."

2. Briefly explain the belief system known as "Romanticism," as you understand it.

3. In what ways is Romanticism a dangerous belief system? How does Satan use it to ensnare us?

4. What practices do we engage in today that can be said to have their influence in Romanticism, or the occult?

5. In your own words, explain Deuteronomy 29:29.

6. Why did Much-Afraid consider continuing her journey without the Shepherd? What did she discover?

Conclusion

Each of us has a path marked out for us that God, in His Sovereignty, has determined is the best path for our lives. It is not the intent of God that we should try to start or complete our pilgrimage without Him. Everything that we will need for our unique pilgrimages has already been allotted to us. Our Shepherd will not withhold one good thing from us that will assist us on our journey, as long as we walk uprightly before Him.

Along our journey, we must remember to line up our desires with the Savior's desires for us, and those desires will ultimately bring Him the most glory. In so doing, we will not be disappointed when He chooses not to give us something that is not good for us, or that will result in detours that end up in costly delays or disaster. Our contentment with the Lord's desires for our lives will serve as a safe-guard against demonic intrusion upon our ear gates.

Applying God's Principles in Our Daily Lives

Points to Ponder

- In our innermost being, we truly desire to trust the Lord and believe that He has our best interests at heart, but life's setbacks, many times caused by our own disobedience, can make us feel as though God has slighted us. Can you think of a time when you felt like God was holding out on you? How did you respond, and how will you respond in the future?

Commit to Prayer

- The Word of God reminds us that "Godliness with contentment is great gain" (1 Tim. 6:6). There are times when we feel that being godly is simply not enough. Our passions, our fleshly cravings cry out for something other than godliness. Those carnal cravings deceive us into believing that the "other than" is "more than." We reason that God does not understand our real needs. We have second guessed the Lord and struck out on our own, hoping to find the great gain and contentment that we desire—apart from Him. If this has been your confession, ask the Lord to forgive you and cleanse your heart from an independent and lustful spirit.
- Confess to the Lord how much you need His presence with you as a guide throughout your life. Surrender your desires to Him once again, and receive His grace to accept, and to truly believe that His plans for you are "to prosper you and not to harm you, plans to give you a hope and a future" (Jer. 29:11).

Part Three

The Eye Gates

Chapter 4

Do You Wish To See?

> If we could only pull out our brain and use only our eyes.
> ~ Pablo Picasso

Chapter Theme

- The purpose of an optical illusion is to fool us into thinking our eyes see something they do not. Optical illusions distort reality through size, shape, color, design and dimension, and even through our own desire to be deluded. Adam and Eve's failure to guard the gates to their ears and eyes made it possible for Satan to create an optical illusion by first distorting the dimension of the garden of Eden itself. With a lie whispered into Eve's ear, he was able to make the garden of Eden appear smaller than it was, and limited in what it could offer her.

For any optical illusion to be effective, the person viewing the illusion must willingly surrender their eyes to the illusion, to some degree. A command must be given to the brain to loosen, or relax its control over what the eyes see so that the illusion can be received. In other words, we have to desire to be fooled by the illusion. In essence, isn't this what we do when we allow the disappointments with life, physical or emotional pain, or even disappointment with God to distort the way that we see our loving Savior? We must ask ourselves if we want to continue to see God through a distorted lens, or if we earnestly desire to have our sight restored.

Do You Wish To See?

Questions for Discussion

1. _____% of the body's sense receptors are located in the retina.

2. Physiologists record that _____ _____ is the single most sensitive of all the human sensory organs.

3. "The eye is the _____ of the _____. If your eyes are good, your whole body will be _____ of _____. But if your eyes are bad, your whole body will be _____ of _____." (Cite the scripture and verse).

4. According to Ackerman, what is the primary function of the eye?

5. Why are optical illusions such enigmas?

6. What causes us to mold a god with our own hands? In your own words briefly explain why this is dangerous for us to do.

7. Often, in the midst of our pain we prefer our _____ because it becomes our _____, or a cover for the irresponsible course of action that we may choose to take,

using our pain to excuse wayward behavior. In what way does John 3:19-21 speak to this issue?

8. What one important question does Jesus ask the paralyzed man in John 5:6?

9. What was the request of the two blind men in John chapter 3?

10. Circle one: True or False

    When we get to the place where we are finally ready to have our sight restored it will be a lot easier than we think.

11. On our own, we are ___ _____ for Satan. It is crucial that we learn how to appropriate the help of the Holy Spirit, asking Him to teach us how to effectively use every weapon in our _____ _____.

12. One act of deliberate strength that goes against our divided will, in the midst of a brutal attack, can _____ _____ _____ _____.

13. What is the promise of God from Isaiah 28:6?

Do You Wish To See?

14. Circle one: True or False

    What moved Eve to ultimately take action against the command of God was what she saw.

15. What was the optical illusion involving the piece of fruit that made it so desirable to Eve?

16. After her conversation with the serpent, Eve began to: [Choose one].
    a) believe a serpent and doubt God
    b) feel like she was missing something
    c) feel like God was keeping something from her to which she was entitled
    d) doubt that she was completely free
    e) all of the above

17. List some of the ways that we err today by locking eyes with this same enticing spirit from Satan.

18. Whatever is hoisted up at the eye gates is what operates in the _____ of _____.

19. What is the second building material needed in the reconstruction of our gates?

Conclusion

Many times, the things we see, or fail to see about God, about our assigned lot in life, or concerning others, are filtered through a lens clouded by the pain of our past or present circumstances. Depending on how we have appropriated the grace of God in the midst of our suffering, we will either accept both good and evil from the Sovereign hand of our wise and loving Creator, or we will feel as though we are being slighted or cheated by God. Failure to guard our gates opens the door for discontentment to find a place in our hearts. We begin to consider and believe the lies that our Adversary plants in our minds. We begin to doubt the Word of the Lord spoken to us. Our eye gates come down, and we begin to peruse the land to consider the optical illusions that Satan has strategically placed just outside the gates.

If we continue to fix our gaze upon these illusions, the result will be a spiritual blindness shrouded in deep, deep darkness. We run the risk of getting lost in the illusions, and being unable to discern the illusion from the reality. Even more debilitating is the risk that we run of ultimately preferring the illusion over reality.

Do You Wish To See?

Applying God's Principles in Our Daily Lives

Points to Ponder

- Can you think of a time when you preferred to believe the optical illusion that Satan presented to you over the reality that you knew to be true? How did you finally break free from that distortion of reality, and what was the lesson learned?
- How does understanding how the brain controls what we see affect how you will choose to view things in the future?
- If we misappropriate the grace of God, blindness, both spiritual and physical, can appear to provide benefits for us that, in actuality, only further handicap us. As you are honest with God, have you ever used your choice to remain spiritually blind as an excuse to justify ignoble, or immature behavior?

Commit to Prayer

- Ask the Lord to reveal and remove any blind spots you might have that are preventing you from seeing Him clearly. Confess the things in your heart that have led you to, first of all, open yourself up to the illusion, and second, to prefer the illusion over reality.
- Meditate on Isaiah 6:1-3, Psalm 27:4-9, Psalm 123:1-2, and Psalm 141:8-10 as you set your gaze upon Him and re-estab-

lish His position of authority over the affairs of your heart and life.

Chapter 5

<u>A Holy Gaze</u>

"They shall look upon Him whom they have pierced."
John19:37, (NKJV)

Chapter Theme

- What we fix our eyes upon is ultimately what we will begin to reflect. If we do not guard our eye gates, we will find ourselves gazing intently upon the deceptions and perversions of truth. While we are distracted, the Enemy seizes the opportunity to stick his foot in the door, and before we even realize it, we too are buying into the lies. The lamp of our body will quickly become flooded with darkness. Suddenly, what was outright sin to us before, now doesn't seem or look so bad, but rather becomes tolerable, and we eventually cease to cry out against it.

We neglect spending time in the presence of God to receive His insight on matters for prayer, therefore we err in our praying. We forget that our vision is impaired and influenced by our own inability to see beyond what we "think we see."

A Holy Gaze

Questions for Discussion

1. What was wrong with the bride in this chapter?

2. What you fix your gaze upon is what you will ultimately _____ to _____.

3. What do the statistics say about Christians viewing pornography?

4. What is the blessed hope of 2 Corinthians 3:18?

5. Why was Jesus not able to be tempted by Satan through his eye gates?

6. When we set our gaze upon the Lord we are drawing _____.

7. What is the third building material for our gates?

8. Why is it difficult for us to see both spiritual and natural truths clearly on our own?

Who's Guarding the Gates? Study Guide

9. Eve saw a piece of fruit disguised as something that could give her a new level of freedom, and promote her to the status of being equal to God. Eve failed to: [Choose one].
   a) see the provision of a loving God in all that comprised her world
   b) see the freedom that she already enjoyed, the peace and the comfort that God had given to her
   c) see the serpent for who he was
   d) see God for who He is
   e) all of the above

10. With our best sight, 20/20 vision, we only see _____ _____ _____ _____ _____.

11. How do we gain spiritual insight into the matters for prayer?

12. What does it mean to stand in the council of the Most High, and what is the benefit to us in prayer when we do?

13. What does John 5:19 say?

14. What is the lesson Jesus wants us to learn from Isaiah 11:3-4?

15. What do the Greek words *optanomai* and *horao* mean?

16. What is the fourth building material for our gates?

Conclusion

The blessed hope of 2 Corinthians 3:18 is this: the more we fix our gaze upon the Beloved Savior, the more we will reflect that same beauty and glory. As the Bride of Christ, we must know Him intimately to know how to dress for our Groom. What we feast our eyes upon continuously is what we will begin to desire and reflect. Unholy desires can lead us away from God and into the throes of sin. We must maintain a holy gaze upon the Savior and upon the Word of God to escape the snares of the devil.

Applying God's Principles in Our Daily Lives

Points to Ponder

- The world that we live in is geared towards visually stimulating our senses by hoisting up images before our eyes that are larger than life for us to feast upon. Daily, the media prepares a table before us with the choicest of obscene delicacies. Ask yourself what you have been feasting your eyes upon as of late. Is the table that you have been feasting from

- one that you would, unashamedly invite the Holy Spirit to feast at alongside you?
- Can you think of a time when you have hurried in to pray over a situation without first hearing clearly from God as to how to pray about it? Explain your experience. How will you respond the next time you witness a situation that you know requires prayer?
- Have you ever considered how fixing your gaze upon those things that are obscene or perverted has the power to alter your physical appearance and your spiritual makeup? Explain. What would you be willing to do to prevent this from occurring again?

Commit to Prayer

- David said in Psalm 101:3, "I will set no vile thing before my eyes." If you have been beholding the vile and the obscene, ask the Lord to forgive you and to cleanse your eyes of everything that has entered your eye gates that offends Him.
- Ask the Lord to strengthen you to change habits that you might have taken on that hold you captive to viewing things that are unholy or offensive to the holiness of God. Meditate on Psalm 101:3, Psalm 25:15; Matthew 5:29; and 2 Corinthians 3:18.

Chapter 6

__A Faulty Lamp__

"The lamp of the wicked will be put out." Proverbs 13:9 (NKJV)

Chapter Theme

- Our Lord has entrusted us to carry His light. However, there are many things that can influence the wattage of our lamps—compromise, lusts, rage, jealousy, fear, pride and rebellion, to name a few. We must be very careful of the unchecked sins that we allow to enter and take up permanent residence in our lives, lest the lamp of our bodies be put out completely, as Proverbs 13:9 says will happen to the lamp of the wicked.

Who's Guarding the Gates? Study Guide

A Faulty Lamp

Questions for Discussion

1. We have been entrusted with God's light and so we must let it shine in our homes, our communities, and to the nations. Yet if we are not careful to guard our eye gates, then what pulses through the currents of our temples, that is, our bodies, will _____.

2. Many of the prophets of old were rendered _____ to God because they walked in agreement with the spirit of _____.

3. _____, _____, _____, _____, _____, _____, _____ and _____, the _____ were true _____ who allowed God to speak to them and paid a high price for walking in the Spirit's boldness and power.

4. What does Proverbs 29:25 say?

5. When our eyes become covetous we will compromise the truth in exchange for _____ _____.

A Faulty Lamp

6. What does Proverbs 28:21 mean to you?

7. For what did Esau sell his birthright?

8. What are some of the modern day tragedies of the spirits of envy, jealousy, anger, and rage?

9. We dress up all of this murderous activity by referring to them as _____ of _____, but in actuality, they are _____ _____. It's really the Devil doing what he does best, _____, _____ and _____.

10. Hanna's story is one of victory and triumph. Why? Briefly explain.

11. Hanna understood the power of _____. Her belief that she was _____ than Peninnah, is what kept her free from envy and looking to God for Him to do for her according to the desire of her own heart.

12. What was Saul's tragic character flaw?

13. Saul's fears led him to operate in _____ and _____ to God.

14. 1 Samuel 18 says, "Saul _____ _____David.

15. How do we respond when pride is operating in our hearts?

16. What can we do as a safeguard against the spirits of jealousy and pride that haunted Saul?

Conclusion

To maintain a bright and pure lamp, we must trust God with our unique assignments within the body of Christ. There must be a level of contentment within us with where we are, and with what God has given each of us to do. We must exercise integrity and love as we render service unto the Lord. It is also important that we learn how to encourage others in their respective areas of talent and giftedness. This will result in joy and peace for us, and God will be both pleased and glorified.

A Faulty Lamp

Applying God's Principles in Our Daily Living

Points to Ponder

- The spirits of compromise, lust, envy, hatred, rebellion, pride, jealousy, and fear can all make the lamps of our bodies flicker on and off until they ultimately go completely out. Take inventory of your life to see if any of these sins are besetting you and causing your lamp to flicker on and off. Once you have identified the cause of your faulty lamp, put a radical plan into action that will not only keep your lamp burning steadily, but also challenge you to make your lamp burn brighter than it ever has before.
- Have you ever experienced the jealous eye from someone, either in the workplace or in the church? How did it affect your performance in that environment? Be prepared to share your experience, as well as discuss ways that perhaps you could have responded better to the situation.
- Find someone whose gift you admire, and tell them how much you appreciate their contribution to the workplace, your family, or the church.

Commit to Prayer

- We must take seriously the responsibility of maintaining the purity of our eye gates. If we constantly find ourselves struggling with faulty lamps, then we are undoubtedly missing out on so much that God intends for us to have and to do. We are robbing ourselves of the joy and peace that God wants us to have as we serve Him, and we are missing out on the enjoyment that we experience when we celebrate the achievements of others as they strive to give God their best service.

- Take some time to examine yourself as you pray this week, and ask the Holy Spirit to show you what is making your lamp go dim. Be quick to agree with Him as He reveals your trouble spots, and then confess the sin, and seek His help and guidance in purifying your lamp. As you pray, thank God for your uniqueness as well as for the gifts and abilities that others bring to the kingdom. Acknowledge that it is God Himself who, in His sovereignty and wisdom, has seen fit to bless each person in the body of Believers according to His good pleasure. Thank Him for this, too.

Part Four

The Heart Gate

Chapter 7

<u>Bring Him the Broken Pieces</u>

Spirit of God, descend upon my heart;
Wean it from earth; through all its pulses move;
Stoop to my weakness, mighty as Thou art;
And make me love Thee as I ought to love.
Hast Thou not bid me love Thee, God and King?
All, all Thine own, soul, heart and strength and mind.
I see Thy cross; there teach my heart to cling:
O let me seek Thee, and O let me find!
Teach me to feel that Thou art always nigh;
Teach me the struggles of the soul to bear.
To check the rising doubt, the rebel sigh,
Teach me the patience of unanswered prayer.
Teach me to love Thee as Thine angels love,
One holy passion filling all my frame;

The kindling of the heaven descended Dove,
My heart an altar, and Thy love the flame

(Spirit of God Descend Upon My Heart Composer – George Croly 1780-1860)

Chapter Theme

- Ask any person you meet if they have ever been heartbroken and they will likely say, "Yes." Ask them what they have done to ensure that their damaged hearts were restored to a healthy, whole state, and most of them will probably say, "Nothing really. I just moved on. Time heals all wounds." But a broken, wounded, and scarred heart needs the healing hands of God upon it to be made completely whole. He alone understands our hearts. We must be willing to bring Him all the pieces so that all of the pieces can be healed. Because all of the issues of life flow out of our hearts, according to Proverbs 4:23, it is important that all of the channels through which they flow are clean. It is from a pure heart that we cry out to God and receive the answers to our prayers.

Bring Him the Broken Pieces

Questions for Discussion

1. Circle one: True or False

    God will heal our broken, scarred, and marred hearts. All we need to do is bring Him our most recent hurts.

2. Name a type of prayer to which God will respond.

3. What does Proverbs 4:23 say?

4. In its original biblical context, what is the definition of the word "issues?"

5. Our boundaries are defined by the virtues that we cultivate, such as _____, _____, _____ and _____.

6. Complete the following sentence:

    Seventeenth century physicians believed that if a person sustained an injury to the heart_____ .

7. The heart was regarded as the _____ of the body.

8. In what ways could Bobby have responded to his broken heart that would have allowed him to experience God on a richer, deeper level?

9. Bobby demanded to know why God had seen fit to take away what he felt he was _____ to have.

10. According to "Father Facts," what percentage of African-American children can expect to spend a significant portion of their childhoods living without their biological fathers?
    Circle one:
    a) 40%
    b) 60%
    c) 80%

11. How did the author's failure to guard her heart gate result in damage to her daughter's heart gate?

12. What is the fifth building material that we cannot afford to leave out in the rebuilding of our gates?

Conclusion

The heart, once considered an enigma to seventeenth century physicians, is no enigma to God. Though it is deceitful and desperately wicked, still God understands every facet of it. Every injury that our hearts have sustained, God knows about it. Every violation to its borders, God is aware of it. Every tear, every puncture, every scar, He sees, He knows and He heals. It is our responsibility to acknowledge those hurts and bring them to God for His healing touch so that our prayers are not negatively influenced by what overflows from our wounded hearts.

Applying God's Principles in Our Daily Living

Points to Ponder

- When was the last time you experienced a move of the Spirit of God upon your heart that led you to a place of true brokenness? What did that brokenness mean to your spiritual growth, and how can you continue to cultivate the kind of brokenness that leads to spiritual maturity?
- What kinds of things can you do to guard your heart gate?

Commit to Prayer

- When we have experienced injury to our hearts, it is important that we bring those hurts to God for healing. Have you been wounded and yet refused to acknowledge those hurts and bring them to God so that your heart could be restored? If yes, take some time today to bring those hurts to God and ask for His healing touch. (See Jer. 30:16-17)
- If your wounds have put you in a place where you have compromised your virtues and are no longer certain of what your boundaries are, or should be, repent of those areas of compromise and ask the Lord to re-establish your borders. (See Ps. 31:1-8; Ps. 16:5-8)
- Because we speak out of the overflow of what is in our hearts, unhealed hurts to our hearts can cause us to speak those things that are grievous to God and to others. Ask the Lord to heal your heart completely so that what proceeds from your mouth is pleasing to Him, and spiritually edifying to others. (See Ps. 19:12-14)

Chapter 8

A Holy House

There must be a work of God in destruction before we are free. We must invite the cross to do its deadly work within us. ~ A.W. Tozer

Chapter Theme

- The closer we get to God the more we see of His holiness and of our filthiness. We know that we are moving beyond Outer Court mentality when we begin to burn and yearn to be made holy as our God is Holy. We see the Lover of our souls and His desire for us, and our love for Him moves us to want to be like Him.

Who's Guarding the Gates? Study Guide

A Holy House

Questions for Discussion

1. What does 1 Corinthians 6:19-20 mean to you? Briefly explain.

2. Match the following:
    a) Outer Court ___. soul
    b) Holy Place ___. spirit
    c) Holy of Holies ___. body

3. In what ways do we know that we are maturing in our relationship with God? [Choose one].
    a) we freely allow His Spirit to move upon our hearts to reveal its true condition
    b) we are stirred from our complacency, and no longer satisfied with the status quo
    c) we burn with an unquenchable desire to move from *where* we are to become more than *what* we are
    d) we will not be happy with less than God's highest goal for us
    e) we yearn and hunger for holiness more than we labor for temporary happiness
    f) all of the above

A Holy House

4. Complete the following sentence:

   God's presence near to us means that He will _____

   _____ .

5. Isaiah 4:4 says that God will come to us as a "_____ of _____" to burn the filth off of us.

6. How do you understand Philip Yancy's statement about our "unworthiness" as it relates to drawing near to God for prayer? Briefly explain. Cite the scripture that substantiates Yancy's statement.

7. Briefly explain what is meant by a heart that is "perfect towards God"?

8. What causes us to miss the visitation of Holy Spirit?

Conclusion

The process of becoming a Holy House is a painful one that requires faith to wait on God and to believe that He will grant us the reward of the one who diligently seeks Him. The benefits of waiting on God and of drawing near to Him are numerous, but among them is the promise from God to perfect that which concerns us, and to make us holy, as He is holy.

In Philippians 2:12, we see that God calls us to work out our own salvation with fear and trembling. This lets us know that there is an expectation from God that we challenge ourselves to be in a state of progression towards perfecting holiness. We progress towards holiness as we cultivate sensitivity to the visitation of the Holy Spirit's movement upon our hearts. This comes from waiting on God, from being still in His presence. From the posture of waiting in faith, we receive a revelation of the holiness of God, and of our own depravity and inability to clean ourselves up. When we do our part, the Holy Spirit does His work of sanctification in our lives.

Applying God's Principles in Our Daily Living

Points to Ponder

- A.W. Tozer says that "there must be a work of God in destruction" in us before we are free. In what area(s) of your life do you sense the Holy Spirit's work of destruction taking place? Are you experiencing liberation from worthless things? How are you progressing towards holiness in these areas?
- At certain points in our walk with God, the Holy Spirit will begin to nudge us to move, to make spiritual progress, and to mature. Take some time over the next week to quiet your spirit and try to discern where the Holy Spirit has been moving upon your heart with a challenge to come closer to

the holiness of God. Keep a journal of what you are discerning. Write down the worthless thing(s) that He is asking you to be rid of.

Commit to Prayer

- In Malachi 3:2-4, we are made aware that when the Holy Spirit comes into our midst, He is coming for judgment to purify us from everything unclean. In your prayer time this week, ask the Lord to reveal the areas of uncleanness in your life to you. Couple your prayer with fasting. Try to pinpoint the single most important area that you believe the Lord would have you focus on. Find scripture that will help you to battle and to prevail over this area of sin in your life. Pray these scriptures over your life daily until you begin to see real progress. Keep a journal of your progress.

Chapter 9

<u>Let's Play Dress-Up!</u>

Surely what a man does when he is taken off guard is the best evidence for what sort of a man he is. What pops out before the man has time to put on a disguise is the truth. If there are rats in a cellar you are most likely to see them if you go in very suddenly. But the suddenness does not create the rats: it only prevents them from hiding. ~ C.S. Lewis

Chapter Theme

- Christians are supposed to live lives that reflect the character of Jesus Christ. For us to do this, we must be willing to take up our cross, deny ourselves, and follow Jesus. We will have to make daily sacrifices in our Christian walk, and this is what often causes many of us to hide our lamps under a bushel, and pretend, like Peter, that we do not know the

Savior (Matt. 26:72). In our hearts, we really desire to be imitators of Christ and live vibrant lives that boldly testify to the saving grace of God, but for many, the price to really live holy is one that is simply too high a price to pay.

This is why we need the help of the Holy Spirit. As we draw closer to Him and develop a deeper intimacy with the Savior, He will empower us to live courageously and authentically for Him.

Who's Guarding the Gates? Study Guide

<u>*Let's Play Dress-Up!*</u>

Questions for Discussion

1. Complete the sentence:
   In our hearts, we want to be like Jesus, but are not willing to pay _____.

2. What is the very first piece of furniture that we encounter in the Outer Court?

3. In the Old Testament, an altar always symbolized the _____ _____ _____ _____.

4. Jesus' public death reminds us that the Outer Court demands a _____, _____ _____ from each of us.

5. What are some of the signs that we are displaying an Outer Court mentality?

6. Complete the sentence:
   The process of rebuilding the gates to our hearts begins with our _____.

74

Let's Play Dress-Up!

7. What is Satan's purpose for using distractions in our lives as it relates to the Outer Court mentality?

8. How do the words of Revelation 11:1-2 affect you? Briefly explain.

9. What did the Lord say to the Laodiceans?

10. What does John 10:17-18 mean to Christians?

11. What is the advantage of having the Lord close to us in times of adversity?

12. Cite the scripture and verse: "These people draw near to me with their mouths, but their hearts are far from me."

13. In our most authentic apparel, how would we be dressed?

Conclusion

The true Christian's life is a life characterized by holiness and consecration. When we live in this manner, we are living as true ambassadors of Jesus Christ and of the kingdom of God. Our focus is not on the superficiality of this world, spending countless hours dressing up our externals in an effort to feel better about what is already wasting away. While it is important that we care for our earthly bodies, we must be ever mindful that God is more concerned about how we dress our inner man. If we will come to Him in faith and trust, He will help us become strong in our faith and authentic in our Christianity.

Applying God's Principles in Our Daily Lives

Points to Ponder

- Have you ever, or are you currently engaged in Outer Court mentality, playing dress-up? How can you challenge yourself to become more authentic in your Christian walk?
- Christians must make daily sacrifices for holiness and righteousness' sake. Have you ever considered any aspect of Christianity too high a price to pay? What steps did, or do you need to take to live out your faith courageously and sacrificially?

- There are many things we can indulge in today that can keep us distracted from and blinded to the deeper requirements of our faith. If you are currently distracted from building intimacy with God, and from progressing in your calling, what would you be willing to do to rid your life of the distractions, change your course, and get back on track with God?

Commit to Prayer

- This week, seek the Lord's help in becoming a more sober-minded Christian (1 Pet. 1:13-16). Challenge yourself to go deeper by searching out scriptures that instruct you to deny your flesh (Luke 9:23), encourage you to live according to the Spirit (Gal. 2:20), and exhort you to put off the deeds of your flesh (Gal. 5:16-26). Spend time meditating on those scriptures.
- Ask the Lord to wash you in His blood and to clothe you in His robe of righteousness. Seek His forgiveness for the areas of pretense in your faith. Ask Him to strengthen you and to build you up so that you can let your light shine brightly and be a bold witness for Him.

Chapter 10

<u>Good Tree – Good Fruit!</u>
<u>Bad Tree – Bad Fruit!</u>

If conversion to Christianity makes no improvement in a man's outward actions – if he continues to be just as snobbish or spiteful or envious or ambitious as he was before – then I think we must suspect his "conversion" was largely imaginary. ~ C.S. Lewis

Chapter Theme

- Have you ever wondered how it is possible for a person to be loving, patient, and compassionate one minute, and ranting, and raving like a mad person the next? It is because the root of their tree has not been made good. In this chapter, we will discuss the importance of allowing ourselves to be vulnerable to the healing hand of God that comes to rescue us from the shame of rotten fruit, and to heal us to enable us to bear good fruit.

Good Tree – Good Fruit! Bad Tree – Bad Fruit!

Questions for Discussion

1. In your own words, briefly tell what you believe C. S. Lewis meant in his quote about a man's conversion.

2. What is the sixth building material necessary in the reconstruction of sound gates?

3. What does Matthew 12:33 say? Write out the scripture.

4. Finish the sentence:
   The Spirit of truth will have us deal truthfully with the _____ and _____ of our being at the present moment so that we are certain to stay in the _____ of _____ more and more into the image and likeness of our Lord.

5. What is the definition of the Greek word *hupomeno*?

6. Circle One: True or False
   It's that radical decision that we make, to go with God, in the face of our greatest opposition and our deepest pain that gets the devil to back off and leave us alone.

7. According to Luke 11:22, what will it take to overcome and dispossess the "strong man?"

8. What happens when a wounded physician ignores his own wounds and tries to administer healing to another's wound?

9. Sometimes God has to take us out of a sin-infested environment and just flat out _____ us.

10. Circle One: True or False

    God's quarantine means that we can certainly trust Him to heal us without having to change our environment, habits, or the people with whom we associate.

11. What does Isaiah 52:11 say?

12. What happens to an open wound?

13. What does John 15 say about the kind of fruit that Jesus wants us to bear?

14. What are the seventh and eighth building materials for our gates?

Conclusion

A fruit-bearing tree makes a statement that one passing by can receive nourishment and strength by eating from it. As Christians, we make that same statement to those with whom we interact. However, when the fruit on our trees, viewed from a close range, looks poor and shriveled and gives off a foul odor, then we must realize it is time for a close inspection of our roots. Even worse, when the fruit that is eaten from our trees results in illness to the partaker, we must get radical about tearing up the root to uncover what is growing there and allow the Holy Spirit, our Tree Surgeon, to perform surgery on our roots.

The goal is to be what we say we are: Christians, good fruit-bearers. God will help us reach our goal, but we must be willing to endure whatever corrective surgery is needed to rid our trees of all its bad produce.

Applying God's Principles in Our Daily Lives

Points to Ponder

- Do you know what is at the root of your tree? Have you ever sat quietly in the presence of the Lord and asked Him to inspect your roots? What would He find if He did?

- Can you recall a time when you tried to help someone else with their issue(s) only to discover that you had the same issue(s)? How did you resolve the conflict in your own soul?

Commit to Prayer

- Begin by thanking God for His commitment to perfecting those things in you that need perfecting. Thank Him for being the Vinedresser, and for pruning you to bear good fruit. (See John 15:1-17)
- Confess anything that you are aware of that is resulting in the production of bad fruit. Ask the Holy Spirit to deal with your roots, to upturn them and to search your heart to reveal any unforgiveness. Ask Him to make you aware of any old wounds that have not been healed or of any bitterness that has taken root there. Ask Him to cleanse you and wash you under His blood, and to heal you completely. (See Ps. 51)
- Finally, ask the Lord to guide you and to help you plant new, healthy roots that will produce a healthy crop of fruit. (See Hos.10:12; Ps. 32:8)

Chapter 11

__Thy Will Be Done__

> There are two kinds of people: those who say to God,
> "Thy will be done," and those to who God says,
> "All right, then, have it your way." ~ C.S. Lewis

Chapter Theme

- If the gates to our hearts are going to be rebuilt solidly and correctly, then we must allow God to have His way in our hearts. There must be a surrendering of every thought pattern and habit that keeps us hiding from the eyes of God. God loves us so much that He will rip one of His good curtains clean down the middle if He feels that we will be content to hide behind it. He wants to see us up close, and so He lovingly prepares the way for us to draw near—flaws and all.

Thy Will Be Done

Questions for Discussion

1. Circle One: True or False

    According to the author, it is best for us to wait for our giants to get really close to our gates before we launch an attack.

2. Our _____ and _____ are the qualifiers that untie the hands of God and allow Him to release power and strength to us to carry out our heart's desire to be made whole.

3. Cite the scripture and verse:

    Solomon said, "There is a way that seems right to a man, but in the end it leads to death."

4. The Holy Spirit's confrontational truth has no mercy. It has but one purpose, and that is _____ .

5. What does Romans 11:32 say?

6. Seventeenth century physicians had discovered that "_____ ."

7. What happens when we choose to depend upon our mental skills to deliver us rather than on the help of the Holy Spirit?

8. What is the warning found in Philippians 3:3?

9. How does the habit of exalting the mind as Lord parallel to the physical malady of the heart known as *arteriosclerosis*?

10. What scripture warns us that when we choose to follow the stubborn inclinations of our evil hearts, we can only go backwards (into captivity) and not forwards?

11. What does Jesus say in Matthew 26:39?

Conclusion

When the searchlight of God's truth confronts our lives, we must make a decision to come out of hiding, abandon our old ways, and let the Lord have His way in and through us. The energy and time we spend hiding behind the deceptions and masks, attempting to figure things out on our own, only wastes precious time and keeps us unnecessarily trapped behind the Enemy's gates. We ensnare ourselves by holding on to our old stubborn ways, knowing that our way is keeping us defeated and enslaved.

In His most agonizing moment, Jesus prayed to the Father, "My Father, if it is possible, may this cup be taken from me. Yet, not as I will, but as You will" (Matt. 26:39). We must be willing to surrender our will and pray that same prayer when we are tempted to have our own way, so that God can begin rebuilding the gates to our hearts and deliver us victoriously into our divine destiny in Him.

Applying God's Principles in Our Daily Lives

Points to Ponder

- How difficult has it been, or is it now, for you to fully surrender the gates to your heart to the Lord? What is it that is making total surrender difficult for you? How has this chapter helped you to overcome that barrier and break free from behind the Enemy's gates?
- What wounds have you suffered that have caused a calcification to form around your heart? How has this affected your witness for Jesus Christ to your family members, coworkers, strangers, and brothers and sisters in the body of Christ?
- How do you think your witness for Jesus Christ would be affected if you could totally surrender your will to His? What are you willing to do to get to that place of freedom and victory?

Commit to Prayer

- The Word of God delivers us into freedom by revealing the truth to us. God's Word has the power to sanctify us. (See John 8:36 and John 17:17) Find at least two other scriptures to meditate on this week that will help you embrace God's truth and walk in greater levels of surrender to His will. Spend time praying those scriptures back to the Lord and into your own heart.
- Thank the Lord for His great mercy and loving-kindness towards you. Meditate on Lamentations 3:22-26.

Part Five
The Mouth Gate

Chapter 12

The Words We Speak

Silence teaches us to speak. A word that is not rooted in silence is a weak and powerless word that sounds like a "clashing cymbal or a booming gong" (1 Cor. 13:1). ~ Henri Nouwen

Chapter Theme

- On average, both men and women speak about 16,000 words a day. What are we talking about? How are those words shaping lives, families, communities, churches, and governments? These are the types of things we must consider when we open our mouths to speak. The power of life and death is in our tongues, and so we must be wise and cautious with the words that we speak (Prov. 18:21).

Who's Guarding the Gates? Study Guide

The Words We Speak

Questions for Discussion

1. What is the wisdom that we can glean from Proverbs 10:19?

2. David _____ _____ _____ of his broken and wounded heart from what he understood as God's divine order and sovereign will.

3. What does Romans 12:14 direct us to do concerning our enemies?

4. Complete the sentence:
God always challenges us, in the toughest legs of our spiritual journey, _____ .

5. What is the admonition from Jesus to us found in John 15:5?

6. Circle One: True or False
If we are angry it is best to simply ignore that anger, pretend that it is not there, and move on.

7. When it is necessary for success, lying is no longer called "lying," but "_____ _____," "_____", and "_____ _____ ."

The Words We Speak

8. What does the Apostle Paul say about those who persist in suppressing truth?

9. As Christians, we must always opt for _____ scaled down to God's holy standards.

10. Write out the words from 1 Corinthians 3:19.

11. How are we empowered to abolish the works of Satan and take possession of his gates?

12. Complete the sentence:
    As we walk in the Spirit, we walk in truth and thereby _____.

13. What is the word of power to us found in Matthew 16:18-19?

14. When we fail to guard the words that we speak, we become nothing more than _____ _____.

15. Our unbridled words can negatively affect the lives of _____ _____ _____ _____.

16. Circle One: True or False

    God is so concerned about our image that He would never ask us to do anything that would make us look foolish in the eyes of others. What scripture do you base your answer on?

17. In light of Ephesians 4:22-32, how should we guard the gates to our mouths?

18. What is the ninth building material in the reconstruction of our gates?

Conclusion

With so much power in our tongues, we need to gain an understanding of the good and the damage that our tongues can do. As we come to the knowledge and appreciation of God's truth, by incorporating that truth into our own lives by embracing it and living it, we become better equipped to use our tongues to take possession of our Enemy's gates. A skilled tongue can significantly shape the kingdom of God for great good.

Applying God's Principles to Our Daily Living

Points to Ponder

- Sixteen thousand words a day is a lot of words flowing from behind the gates to our mouths. Does this statistic make you want to be more careful about what you are saying? What radical steps are you willing to take to guard the gates to your mouth?
- Jesus teaches us in Matthew 5:38-48 about the importance of going the extra mile to bless others, including our enemies. It is easy to bless those we love, but Paul also challenges us to bless the very ones who cause us pain and trouble (Rom. 12:14). How difficult has this commandment been for you to follow? Are you prepared today to bless someone who has been a source of intentional pain and hurt in your life?

Commit to Prayer

- Take some time to meditate on Matthew 5:38-48 and Romans 12:14. Ask the Lord to cleanse your heart of any unforgiveness you may be holding onto against those who have intended evil for you. In prayer, release them from any debt (meaning any apology or retribution) that you feel they may owe you, and then ask the Lord to bless your enemies and open your heart to also be a blessing to them.

- Ask the Lord to make you more conscientious concerning the words that you speak. In prayer, declare Him Lord over the gate to your mouth. Begin to make yourself accountable to Him for every word that you utter. (See Ps. 19:14)

- Put your authority into practice by spending some time declaring the will of God over the marriages of people within your immediate sphere of influence, your own family, the community that you live in, the church you attend, and over our current government. (See Matt. 16:18-19)

Chapter 13

Bent By A Word

A single sentence can be a life sentence ~ Author Unknown

Chapter Theme

- Before the tragedy of Eden, God had empowered mankind to speak words of life over all creation. In Genesis 2, we read where Adam was given the wonderful project of naming every living creature. However, after Adam and Eve disobeyed God, the words that they began to speak were words that started to bend creation towards death. Adam, blaming God and Eve for his disobedience, and Eve blaming the serpent. (Gen. 3:11-13)

We continue to see their destructive use of words in the naming of their first two children – *Cain*, which means, "to provoke to jealousy, chant or wail at a funeral, mourning mother," and *Abel*, which means, "emptiness, transitory, vanity, and unsatisfactory." Both sons, having been bent by their names, lived out the tragic meanings of those names.

With our mouths we can either build up or tear down. We have the power to bend lives, the power to bend our communities, our children, our churches, and our governments, either towards damnation or redemption.

Bent by a Word

Questions for Discussion

1. Complete the quote:

   "A single sentence _____."

2. What do the Hebrew names "Cain" and "Abel" mean?

3. In what ways were both Cain and Abel bent in the direction of their names? Briefly explain.

4. What happens when a mother calls her own child "stupid," "lazy" or "good for nothing?"

5. What did God have to do to Isaiah before He could use him as a mouthpiece for Him?

6. Briefly explain what the words of Proverbs 12:18 mean to you?

7. What does Proverbs 10:18 say?

8. What is the promise to us found in Psalm 15:1-5?

9. What are some of the blessings that we will witness as the saints open their mouths and declare truth?

10. What is the warning to us from Jesus found in Matthew 12:36-37?

11. Complete the sentence:
    At the entrance to every gate
    _____
    _____ .

12. How was Linda's life impacted by a few unwise words spoken by her father?

13. Circle One: True or False
    God is not concerned if we fail to speak up when we should. He is more concerned about what we do say than He is about what we do not say.

14. What is the exhortation to us from both Proverbs 3:27 and Romans 15:1-3?

15. What happened to the one leper who returned to say "Thank you" to Jesus?

16. Jesus said, "If you abide in Me and My words abide in you,

_____

17. What is the tenth building material for strong gates?

Conclusion

An unbridled word can so bend a person that they will struggle their entire lives to reposition themselves from the mangling effects of that word. We must get back to the place where we are using our tongues to resurrect, redeem, strengthen, and encourage one another, as God intended. The only one we should be bending towards damnation is the Devil himself. His doom is sure without our assistance, but a reminder from us to him every now and then is always fitting.

Applying God's Principles in Our Daily Living

Points to Ponder

- Looking back over your life, do you feel you have had to struggle out from under a word or words that have had you bent towards destruction? In what way(s) were you bent? How was redemption worked in your life to reposition you?

- Have you, in turn, ever used words to bend anyone within your sphere of influence? How was that person harmed and what have you done to undo the damage caused by your words? What lesson(s) have you learned from that experience?
- Can you think of a situation where God can use you to help release someone who is in bondage to a harmful word spoken over them?

Commit to Prayer

- Ask the Lord to give you wisdom in the use of your words so that your words will not cause harm or pain to anyone. (See 1 Chron. 4:9)
- Sometimes we fail to say encouraging or strengthening words to others because we are waiting for someone to say them to us first. In prayer, ask the Lord to free you so that your words of encouragement and hope will flow from a heart overflowing with His love, unhindered by outside influences. (See Prov. 11:25 and 3:27)

Chapter 14

<u>Choose Your Battles</u>

He who lives by fighting with an enemy has an interest in the preservation of the enemy's life. ~ Friedrich Wilhelm Nietzsche

Chapter Theme

- As the warfare between good and evil rages in our midst, Christians must engage the Enemy as skilled warriors on the battlefield. We must know who we are in Christ to be effective on the battlefield. We must know what weapons we carry in our arsenal, which battles are ours to fight, and which battles belong to God.

Choose Your Battles

Questions for Discussion

1. In your own words, explain what Friedrich Nietzsche meant in his quote about fighting the enemy?

2. How does Proverbs 23:7 help us gain the right image of ourselves as warriors against evil?

3. When we have been offended, how should we approach our offenders?

4. In your own words, explain how Romans 2:5-6 can help us consider our course of action when offended, and keep short accounts?

5. What does Jesus direct us to do when we encounter repeat offenders? Cite the scripture and verse.

6. How does Ephesians 6:12 enlighten us to whom and what we are really engaging in the battle?

7. Circle One: True or False

    According to Proverbs 19:11: "It is to a man's weakness to overlook an offense."

8. What did God instruct Jehoshaphat to do when he went into battle? What was the outcome of that battle?

9. What did Eli say to himself to avoid an unnecessary confrontation and remain focused on his mission?

10. In his warning to Timothy, what does Paul say about contentious people? Cite the scripture and verse.

11. What does the Lord promise us in Isaiah, chapter 49:25-26?

12. What is the eleventh building material for sturdy gates?

Conclusion

As we wage war against our Adversary, we should always remember that we are engaging a cunning enemy. When we are careful to stick to the path charted for us and take our directions from the Holy Spirit, we avoid unnecessary, and sometimes deadly, confrontations. If we allow Him, our God will fight many of the battles for us. So we must choose our battles wisely to finish our mission victoriously and glorify God.

Applying God's Principles in Our Daily Lives

Points to Ponder

- If we insist on firing back at every enemy every time they fire at us, we will soon run out of stamina and ammunition. If you find yourself experiencing battle fatigue, consider the possibility that some of the battles that you are fighting are actually meant for God to fight. Are you willing to relinquish those battles to Him?
- The Word of God tells us that we will encounter offenses in this world. What has been your response to offenses in the past? If there is room for improvement, how can you improve?
- How good are you at avoiding unnecessary confrontation and confrontational people? If habitually confrontational, or argumentative people are part of your circle of friends and acquaintances, are you willing to change your friends and acquaintances?

Commit to Prayer

- In 2 Chronicles 20, God told Jehoshaphat that all he had to do was to face an enemy who would not go away, and that He (God) would do the fighting for him. As you go before the Father in prayer, ask Him to give you wisdom to know which battles He intends for you to fight, and which ones belong to Him.
- The world is full of offensive people, and we are certain to encounter more than a few of them if we live long enough. If you struggle with the spirit of offense and feel that you need to confront everyone who offends you, ask the Holy Spirit to give you grace to overlook offenses and to trust Him to deal with your offenders in His way and in His time.
- If you have gotten off track by being engaged in needless confrontation, ask the Lord to order your steps and to help you stay faithful to the course that He has charted for you to follow. (See Ps. 37:23; Ps. 119:133-135; Heb. 12:1-3)

Chapter 15

Abiding In Jesus – The Discipline Of Waiting

"Those who wait on the Lord shall renew their strength."

Isa. 40:31

Chapter Theme

- We live in a rapidly paced society that has grown accustomed to having everything quick, fast, and in a hurry. Our time is well consumed with all kinds of technological toys and gadgets that can easily keep us occupied for hours and hours on end. We have allowed the pace of society and the gadgets in our hands, and before our faces, to completely push our Lord out of the frame of our lives. Waiting in the presence of God is almost unheard of these days. In fact, waiting has become a big "No, No," and is punishable by free meals in most fast food restaurants.

We must hasten back to the discipline of waiting in the presence of our Lord. With the rapid moral decline in our nation, now more than ever, Christians need to be able to hear from God to be a consistent voice crying out for righteousness and holiness in the earth.

Abiding in Jesus – The Discipline of Waiting

Questions for Discussion

1. What is the Greek definition of the word *abide*?

2. How has technology alienated us from the presence of God?

3. Complete the sentence:
   Yet the admonition from Jesus is still to "_____ and _____." Cite the scripture and verse.

4. In your own words, briefly explain what Hebrews 11:6 means.

5. What is the definition of the Hebrew word *damam*?

6. Knowing that the Devil is working hard to pull us away from intimacy with our God, our daily prayer should be _____.

7. What does Daniel say will be the reward of the people who remain intimate with the Lord?

8. In Matthew 24:45-46, who does Jesus consider a faithful servant?

9. As believers, what kinds of things can we do to stay active while we wait before the Lord?

10. Circle One: True or False

    Our inactivity does not necessarily mean that we are falling away from Jesus.

11. The gates of our mouths must be as ports harboring _____ and our mouths must be the harbingers of _____ .

12. In what way are we currently being desensitized to the spirit of error and deception?

13. What three things does Jesus say about the Spirit of Truth working on our behalf? Cite the scripture and verses.

14. When we sit for hours on end watching reality television, we are being _____ _____ of the time that God has given to us.

15. Circle One: True or False

    The only ones who really need to be lifting up their voices in prayer against all types of deception are the intercessors.

16. Who was God looking for in Ezekiel 22:30?

17. Besides Jeremiah and possibly Baruch, how many worthy people did the Lord find to stand in the gap? (Ezek. 22:30)

18. What do we need to do to walk in the manifested power of our Holy God?

19. What is the twelfth building material for our gates?

Conclusion

There is no question that we are living in times when the presence of God is urgently needed, and yet little sought after. We have foolishly nudged Him further and further away from the mainstream of our daily activities, and into a cobwebbed, dark, unvisited room in the cellar of our lives. Like self-indulged little children, we have preferred to spend our time interacting with our toys, and indulging ourselves in endless hours of mindless entertainment.

The eyes and the heart of God are on the lookout now. He is searching for those who have a heart to seek Him. He is knocking at

Abiding In Jesus – The Discipline Of Waiting

the door and rattling our gates. He wants back in. He wants to meet us in our prayer closets again. He wants to show up in our devotional time and reveal great and glorious secrets to us as we wait in His presence and meditate on His Word. Even though He tarries in His return, He wants us to stay vibrantly and actively connected to Him while we wait.

Applying God's Principles in Our Daily Lives

Points to Ponder

- How much time do you spend abiding in the presence of God, reading and meditating upon His Word? If the answer to this question disappoints you, how can you improve upon your devotional time?
- How much time do you spend on Facebook and Twitter, texting, or just watching reality TV? Is the amount of time disproportionate to the time that you spend with Jesus? What are you willing to do to bring balance to your life so that you are no longer allowing Satan to consume your time, but rather, the Holy Spirit to dictate the moments of your days?
- Are you aware of the workings of the spirit of error and deception in the world and in your life? After reading this chapter, how will you take a stand against those spirits to

ensure that you are not caught off guard by them, and are suited up in, and undergirded by truth?

Commit to Prayer

- If you have been crowding the Lord out of your life by allowing your time to be consumed with other things, repent now. Ask the Lord to forgive you and to help you exercise more discipline in the area of your devotional time with Him. Ask Him to illuminate His Word to you, and to make His presence known to you as you purposefully set time aside to seek His face.
- Almost on a daily basis, we will encounter some form of deception. As Christians, we are called to be salt and light, to make an impression for Jesus upon an immoral world. If you have had opportunities to be salt and light in the midst of darkness but instead hid your light, ask the Lord to give you boldness to let your light shine. Ask Him to use you to bring glory and honor to His name as you change your world for the sake of His name. (See Matt. 5:13-16)

Chapter 16

<u>Are You Ready to Rumble?</u>

"Blessed be the Lord, my rock, who trains my hand for war, and my fingers for battle." Ps. 144:1

Chapter Theme

- Whether we like it or not, we are all engaged in a war. The battle was already underway when we arrived on the scene from that warm, cozy, comfortable place in our mother's womb. It may be a harsh reality, but from the moment of conception, the battle for our souls began. Wisdom would tell us to prepare for the battle. Our God will equip us with divine strategies against our Adversary. He will train us for war. He will be with our hands and our mouths. He will give us victory on the battlefield as we take possession of the Enemy's gates.

Are You Ready to Rumble?

Questions for Discussion

1 What does Leviticus 26:8 mean to you?

2. An effective strategy that the devil has used upon the body of Christ has been to place a spirit of _____ upon us so that we cannot effectively pray.

3. Many in the body of Christ are _____ doing things that God never _____ _____ _____ _____.

4. What does Jesus say emphatically in John 15:5? Briefly explain what that means to you.

5. List one of the things that we see occurring as a result of our exhaustion?

6. Circle One: True or False
   The minute the Devil sees that there is no daddy seated at His place of authority at the main gate to the family unit, he turns and goes the other way.

Are You Ready to Rumble?

7. What are a few of the effects of the spirit of death permeating our surroundings, our homes, our schools, our streets and our churches?

8. What does Jesus say in John chapter 6:63? Briefly explain what he meant by these words?

9. What is the definition of the two Greek words *gregoreuo,* and *egeiro?*

10. Circle One:

    What approach should we take when we begin to fall asleep while praying?

    a. change your strategy

    b. switch your position

    c. walk and pray

    d. jog and pray

    e. ride your bike and pray

    f. sing your prayer

    g. all of the above

11. The devil is always on the prowl looking for someone who is _____ and _____ to _____.

Who's Guarding the Gates? Study Guide

12. What does the author say is the problem with always praying other people's prayers?

13. What does David say about prayer in Psalm 5:3, Psalm 88:13, and Psalm 19:14?

14. Complete the sentence:
    In the boxing ring, the power is in the punch. In spiritual warfare, the _____.

15. Prayers that are bathed in the Holy Spirit's presence wield ammunition that _____ _____ _____ _____ _____ .

16. That "ho-hum" mentality in prayer indicates that we are _____.

17. 1 John 5:14-15 lets us know that _____.
    _____.

18. Just like the boxer who prepares for a boxing match, we too must be willing to have our tongues _____ - set apart for God's use.

19. What is the thirteenth building material in the reconstruction of our gates?

Conclusion

A soldier on the battlefield without his weapons is a dead soldier. A child of God on the battlefield of spiritual warfare, attempting to do combat with demonic forces without his weapons, is also doomed. He is an easy prey for the Devil who is constantly on the prowl looking for just such a one to tear to pieces. looking for just such a one to tear to pieces. Our God has made us "more than conquerors" and we can stand against the Enemy, battle-ready, when we allow Him to sanctify our mouths. We can overturn the Enemy's death threats to our children, ministries, anointing, churches, and all that he has decreed to die. Instead, with a sanctified tongue we can decree death to his agenda concerning the kingdom of God. Everything that he has knocked unconscious in the ring, God will empower us to revive. Hallelujah!

Applying God's Principles in Our Daily Lives

Points to Ponder

- This week take some time to jot down a list of all the activities that you are involved in. Do two things with that list; first, look at it to see if you have taken on unnecessary tasks, or projects, that the Lord did not intend for you to take on. Next, begin to weed out those activities or projects that were not put on your plate by God. Consider giving the time you have freed up for yourself back to the Lord in the study of His Word and in prayer.

- Are there areas in your home life that you have not been attentive to guard in prayer simply because you have been too exhausted to pray? What strategy will you devise to stand effectively in prayer over those areas?

- Do the kinds of prayers that you pray have devil-knockout power, or are you praying someone else's prayer from a pamphlet every time you kneel down to pray? How can you increase your influence and effectiveness in prayer so that you are wielding blows that will catch the Devil on his blind side?

Commit to Prayer

- Ask the Lord to help you eliminate excessive activity from your life that keeps you too exhausted to pray effectively. Set aside time for prayer, daily, that you will not allow anyone or anything to distract you from, short of a valid emergency.

- Seek the Lord for a greater level of anointing in prayer that will result in answers with visible manifestations. This will glorify God and encourage you and strengthen you in your prayer life.

Part Six

The Mind Gate

Chapter 17

<u>Which Way Did I Go?</u>

If the Lord had not been on our side –

Let Israel say-

If the Lord had not been on our side when men attacked us,

when their anger flared against us,

they would have swallowed us alive;

the flood would have engulfed us,

the torrent would have swept over us,

the raging waters would have swept us away.

Praise be to the Lord,

who has not let us be torn by their teeth.

We have escaped like a bird out of the fowler's snare;

the snare has been broken, and we have escaped.

Ps. 124

Chapter Theme

- Statistics show that one in four individuals suffer from some form of a mental disorder. This chapter examines some of the root causes of these mental disorders, and the resultant behaviors that individuals living with these disorders will face. We will uncover scriptures that deal with the topic of healing, spiritually, physically, and emotionally, and see how important it was to Jesus that the sick be made completely whole.

Which Way Did I Go?

Questions for Discussion

1. Complete the sentence:

    When we say that we believe a thing to be true and yet our living bespeaks quite a different truth, we are _____.

2. In your own words, briefly explain the following quote from the author:

    "The shores that we land upon in the dark nights of the soul will be determined by the truths or the lies that we have either chosen to embrace or to reject in the light."

3. Complete the sentence:

    The holes that are left in our souls through such deep loss cause a part of us to get stuck, or left, in the place _____ _____ _____ _____ _____.

4. What does James 1:8 say?

5. What is the definition of the Greek word *dipsuchos*?

6. What does Jesus say that he came to do, in Luke 4:18?

7. Give the definitions of the Greek words *thraou,* and *agnumi*?

8. How does God's goal for us differ from Satan's when we experience shattering in our lives?
   Give the scripture reference from the book of Romans.

9. Why is it helpful for us to bear in mind the image of the jostled thousand-piece puzzle as we co-exist and co-labor with our brothers and sisters in Christ, and with unbelievers?

10. _____ can make us come unhinged. It can make us _____, _____ and _____ .

11. Circle One:
    Which of the following scriptures encourage us to love each other, flaws and all?
    a) John 15:12-13
    b) 1 Peter 4:8
    c) 1 Corinthians 13
    d) all of the above

12. According to 1 John 3:8, what was the mission of Jesus Christ?

Which Way Did I Go?

13. Circle One:

    Which of the following scriptures lets us know that Jesus wants us to be made completely whole?

    a) Isaiah 53:5

    b) 1 Corinthians 6:17

    c) Psalm 23:3

    d) all of the above

14. What is the fourteenth building material for our gates?

15. Circle One: True or False

    According to Dianne and Robert Hales, only 1 out of every 13 people suffers with a mental disorder.

16. What does Jehovah say about Himself in Exodus 15:26?

17. List some of the contributing factors to mental disorders.

18. The leper in Luke 17:11-19, who returned to tell Jesus, "Thank You," was made completely whole. What do you believe happened to the other nine?

19. What is the definition of the Greek word *sozo*?

Who's Guarding the Gates? Study Guide

20. Circle One: True or False

    It is important for adults, traumatized as children, to continue to hold fast to the resolutions that they made to protect themselves from their abusers while they were only children. Those resolutions will continue to protect them as adults.

21. What commonality is found in Nehemiah 1:3, and some of the lyrics in Gloria Gaynor's song, *I Will Survive*?

22. According to Ezekiel 38, under what conditions does the Devil look and plot to repossess our gates?

23. How does the author draw the parallel between adult survivors of childhood trauma who have neglected their mental health, to being "back in the province," as Nehemiah puts it?

24. Briefly explain the behavior known as the "shutters coming down."

25. List the three coping mechanisms that a child living under traumatizing conditions will employ to survive his surroundings.

    _____   _____   _____ .

26. Circle One: True or False

    Denial says, "This is happening to someone else."

27. Why is it especially important for intercessors to make sure that they are whole before they position themselves in the gap for others?

28. In what scripture does Paul tell us that adults should confront life's challenges as adults?

29. What is the exhortation to us found in Philippians 2:12?

30. What is the fifteenth building material for our gates?

Conclusion

Mental disorders have psychological, medical, biological, and environmental roots. No matter the root cause of the disorder, it is still the will of God that we are made completely whole. We must do whatever is within our power to promote the healing process, knowing that the Holy Spirit will give us the courage to confront our fears along the way. Then, we must trust the "Lord who heals us" to do what only He can do to make us completely whole.

Applying God's Principles to Our Daily Lives

Points to Ponder

- We often fight with others, preferring to blame them for the pain we are experiencing in life, rather than holding the mirror up to ourselves and confronting our own inner demons. Have you taken time for introspection to discover and uncover some personal issues that you have not yet dealt with that are keeping you bound? Are you afraid to confront yourself? If yes, why? If not, why haven't you?
- When we encounter difficult trials in life we tend to either hold onto the promises of God to see us through, or in misjudging God, we will believe a lie from the Enemy, which will dump us onto the shores of a strange kingdom. What lies have you embraced in the dark night of your soul that have caused you to land upon foreign soil?
- Often, we have negative confrontations with others simply because we do not understand their needs or point of view, and they do not seem to understand ours. How will the concept of the thousand-piece puzzle, presented in this chapter, help you to resolve differences and misunderstandings in a more loving and Christ-like manner?

Commit to Prayer

- If you feel that you are still suffering from a "shattering" that touched your life many years ago, ask the Lord to give you the courage to confront yourself and to face the truth about yourself first, before you take action to confront anyone else. (See Ps. 51)
- With the understanding that we are all operating with some form of fragmentation, ask the Lord to help you to exercise more patience, mercy, love, and compassion towards everyone, including yourself.
- Take some time to thank the Lord for understanding your frame and your frailties (See Ps. 103:14). Thank Him for loving you unconditionally, and for being committed to seeing you made completely whole. (See Ps. 103:3; 3 John 2; and Jer. 30:16-17)

Chapter 18

<u>A Candidate for Change</u>

Do not be conformed to this world (this age), [fashioned after and adapted to its external, superficial customs], but be transformed (changed) by the [entire] renewal of your mind [by its new ideals and its new attitude], so that you may prove [for yourselves] what is the good and acceptable and perfect will of God, even the thing which is good and acceptable and perfect [in His sight for you].
Romans 12:2, (Amp)

Chapter Theme

- A damaged mind translates into a damaged life. After all the damage that has been done to destroy the gates to our minds, we will have our work cut out for us when it comes time to repair and rebuild. With God's help, we can surely experience total transformation, but we must be candidates for change, willing to participate in the process that will bring the desired change to our minds. We must have a vision of ourselves in our transformed state, thinking clearly, seeing clearly, walking confidently, living victoriously without bars around us, and without chains holding us down. We must be able to see ourselves changed, healed, restored, and renewed.

Who's Guarding the Gates? Study Guide

A Candidate for Change

Questions for Discussion

1. Complete the sentence:
   Man is only becoming whole while reaching out to other living creatures and concrete things. He can only know himself _____ _____ _____.

2. Circle One: True or False
   Survivors of childhood trauma are very often loners.

3. Briefly explain the *flight or fight* syndrome.

4. What happens when a child trapped in an abusive or traumatizing situation sees that he cannot flee the situation or fight back?

5. Complete the sentence:
   When you make up your mind to regain possession of the gates to your mind, you have set the _____ of _____ in motion over your life.

6. Define "transformation."

A Candidate for Change

7. How does life change for us once we experience transformation?

8. How do we achieve a renewed mind?

9. According to Chris Thurman, what is one of the biggest challenges to becoming mentally whole?

10. Complete the sentence:

    Make a list of the things that you find most difficult to do along your road to recovery, then pick one of them and _____ _____ _____ _____!

11. Complete the sentence:

    The character builders are found _____ _____ _____ to transformation, not in the act of liberation.

12. Circle One: True or False

    If it takes forty years or more for Him to repair our gates and redeem our damaged minds, God will do, in His sovereignty, what is best for us. He will not cut corners because He is in no hurry.

13. What is the promise to us found in Proverbs 28:13?

Conclusion

Trauma, trials, and the vicissitudes of life come as battering rams against the gates to our minds. We can take such a vicious beating, mentally, that we reach overload, and everything in us simply shuts down. We lose touch with who we are and why God placed us on this earth, to the point where we feel hopeless, depressed, isolated, and forgotten. Our mental gates can experience so much devastation that we can forget what it is like to live with peace, joy, and hope for each new day.

It is the goal of Satan to keep us in the place of defeat, but if we will begin to cry out to God to reconstruct our lives by rebuilding the gates to our minds, we will experience the Holy Spirit's help. God wants us to begin to reach for that better place. The Holy Spirit will empower us and strengthen us to participate in the process of wholeness without fear. We have to become radical and even violent with our Adversary, realizing that our minds are the territory that the Devil works hard to possess as his own. He will not give up that ground without a fight. Yet, the hope of being made whole must begin to be our daily expectation as we obediently work in concert with our Lord in the restoration of soundness to our minds.

A Candidate for Change

Applying God's Principles in Our Daily Lives

Points to Ponder

- If you have suffered from a battering to the gates to your mind that drove you to a place of fear, depression, and isolation, search your life to determine whether or not you have been able to come out of that place and reconnect with the world and with people, or are you still feeling disconnected? If you are still feeling disconnected, ask yourself if you have wholeheartedly sought the Lord for a plan of action that will get you outer-focused and help you to become the healthy, whole, and vibrant individual that He created you to be?
- Understanding that the definition of the word "transformation" means to shift, to mutate, a conversion, gradual change, revolution, metamorphosis, and finally, to turn the corner, can you identify an area in your life where you can honestly say that you have, or are now experiencing transformation orchestrated by God? What did you do to get to that place?

Commit to Prayer

- If you are having trouble reconnecting to the world and to people after having suffered a severe attack on your mind, ask the Lord to help you get outer-focused by strengthening you to begin some sort of outreach in your community; e.g., visiting the sick, or going to the nursing home in your city.

- As we have learned in this chapter, one of the greatest barriers to wholeness is that people just do not want to do the hard work that is required to get well. This week, pray that the Holy Spirit will empower you to challenge yourself to do what you have, prior to this moment, considered too hard an undertaking for you on your journey to wholeness. Take steps this week to actually do the hard thing(s) that will get you closer to wholeness. By taking these steps, you will feel empowered and your faith will increase. (See Phil. 2:12)

Chapter 19

My Mind's Made Up

"You knit me together in my mother's womb. I praise you because I am fearfully and wonderfully made." Ps. 139:13-14a

Chapter Theme

- Abba, our Heavenly Daddy, made us and formed us in our mother's wombs, fearfully and wonderfully. However, the presence of sin in our world, which we are exposed to on a daily basis, has the power to warp the beauty of God's creation. God made our minds, a fantastic mechanism, to think on Him, to study Him, to know Him, and to interact with Him as He communicates with us about our purpose and influence on Earth.

The presence of sin and its damaging effects upon our minds have influenced us to choose a path other than that which God intended for us. Negative thought patterns that we have held onto down through the years, and unresolved past issues, will hinder our walk with God and damage others, both in the body of Christ and in the secular community. Because of His great love for us, God will call for a timeout in our lives so that we can decisively deal with the harassing spirits that hinder us and spoil our testimony of victory in Christ.

My Mind's Made Up

My Mind's Made Up

Questions for Discussion

1. Fill in the blank:

   The human brain is like the _____ of the body.

2. What is the function of *synapses*?

3. Circle one: True or False

   Synapses develop throughout life, even into adulthood.

4. What happens to early synapses that are not strengthened and reinforced through repetitive use?

5. With your understanding of the function of synapses, briefly explain why it is difficult for adult survivors of early childhood trauma to undo negative behavior and thought patterns on their own.

6. What the mind thinks determines where the _____ _____ _____ _____ _____ _____.

7. Complete the sentence:

Who's Guarding the Gates? Study Guide

Attempts to build, grow, or advance from a cornerstone built of flesh _____.

8. What is the lesson to us from Zechariah 4:6?

9. Fill in the blanks:

   We must daily seek out and welcome _____, _____, _____ and _____ transformation that only our Redeemer can give.

10. What is the likely reason why an anointed man or woman of God, who seemed to be advancing in ministry, all of a sudden appears to have hit a ceiling and can go no further?

11. Circle one:

    Jesus said of His Father, "Every branch in me that does not bear fruit, He. . .
    a) ignores it
    b) cuts it off
    c) prunes so that it bears more fruit

12. Why does God lead us beside still waters?

13. Fill in the blanks:

    The One who made our minds can _____ and _____ our minds.

14. What happens when the finger of God reaches in and touches the damaged cells in our minds?

15. What is the sixteenth building material for our gates?

Conclusion

God can and will heal us when we bring our sickness to Him and ask Him for healing that only He can give. When we are aware of our own mental ills, and yet we do not seek the Lord for a cure, we are putting ourselves in danger of both having to undergo a radical surgery requiring amputation, and willfully resisting the healing hand of God upon our lives. We must repent of continuing along our own stubborn path and turn to the Lord for forgiveness and healing.

Applying God's Principles in Our Daily Living

Points to Ponder

- In this chapter we learned the function of synapses and how important it is for us to have healthy synapses reinforced early in life. With this understanding, are there any unhealthy behaviors and thought patterns that you still maintain in life and can trace back to the place where your synapses were being developed and reinforced under negative conditions? Knowing that God is our Healer and that He wants us to come to Him for healing, what steps are you willing to take to ensure that you are made completely whole?
- When we make attempts to rebuild our lives completely on our own after we have suffered loss through mental trauma, we will soon discover that we are building upon sinking sand. Psalm 127:1 reminds us that "Unless the Lord builds the house, its builders labor in vain." Have you been trying to heal yourself, by yourself? Have you been trying to fix your life by force of will? How is that working for you? What can you do to change that?

My Mind's Made Up

Commit to Prayer

- If there is an infant or small child in your life, under your care, ask the Lord to help you to build healthy and strong synapses into the brain cells of this child by consistently loving, tenderly touching, and speaking life-giving words over him or her.
- Ask the Lord to help you to be quick to come to Him for healing in any area in your life where a nerve has been left exposed, or where a wound has been only patched up. Repent for continuing on your own way, knowing that you were carrying around diseased parts. (See Ps. 32:3-5; Ps. 41:4; Jer. 17:5-8; Luke 6:17-19)
- Give thanks to the Lord for having mercy on you and for healing all of your soul's diseases. Worship Him for creating you so fearfully and wonderfully, and for having the incredible power to touch and restore your soul.

Chapter 20

Looking Back

"Forgetting those things which are behind and reaching forward to what lies ahead, I press toward the goal for the prize of the upward call of God, in Christ Jesus." Phil. 3:13-14

Chapter Theme

- While Paul exhorts us, in Philippians 3:13-14, to forget the things that are behind us, if our past is still a major hindrance to our present quality of life, then it will most certainly dictate our future quality of life. We only have the luxury of forgetting our past once we have properly dealt with the giants involved in yesterday's struggles. If we have allowed yesterday's giants to follow us into our present, taking possession of our land along the way, then we cannot effectively press on towards the high call of God, in Christ Jesus, unless we are pressing to conquer those giants and to rid them from our land.

Who's Guarding the Gates? Study Guide

Looking Back

Questions for Discussion

1. In Deuteronomy 7, how does God say He will drive out the seven mighty nations?

2. Briefly explain your understanding of Matthew 12:29.

3. Circle one: True or False
   When God delivers us, He wants us to understand exactly what we are being delivered out of and into.

4. What is the seventeenth building material for our gates?

5. In Deuteronomy 7, God names each of these seven giants that must be destroyed before possession of the land can occur. He hands them over to us one at a time, by name, and then commands us to _____ _____ _____.

6. It is in the very _____ of the battle against the giants, against those strongholds in our minds, that deliverance is achieved.

7. Briefly explain some of the underlying reasons why survivors of long-term trauma yoke themselves to toxic relationships, behaviors, and addictions.

8. Complete the sentence:
Many adults who spend most of their childhoods in traumatizing or abusive surroundings, where everything that existed, existed solely on the strength of a lie, evolved from and was held together by a lie, _____ .

9. What will free us from the perceived need to lean or depend upon a lie?

10. What scripture lets us know that God will not allow us to get comfortable with a lie?

11. What are some of the truths about unjust suffering, and God's position on such suffering? Back up your response with at least one scripture.

12. It is the love of God that _____ ____ _____ whenever we undergo unbearable suffering.

Conclusion

When the hand of God is upon us to deliver us, He wants us to be fully aware of what we are being delivered out of and into. The benefit of having a thorough knowledge of the deliverance that God works in our lives is that we are less likely to be ensnared by the same giants again. We will know how to gird ourselves against future attacks. Looking back may be painful, but it is the only way to move forward victoriously.

Applying God's Principles in Our Daily lives

Points to Ponder

- We all want to be free from some bondage to some sin. Our desire is to serve the Lord and to serve others without hindrances. However, in our quest for freedom we must be sure to ask the Lord to grant us deliverance with understanding. Have you been one who stands in the deliverance line week after week without ever really gaining an understanding of what you are being delivered from, or of what lies at the root of your bondage? After reading this chapter, what steps will you take to get to the root of the stronghold in your life?

Looking Back

- Can you identify an "ite," or a "giant" that has hindered your life? How can you take possession of this giant's gates and get him off of your land?
- Have you ever mistaken the silence of God for impotence or indifference? After reading this chapter, how has your attitude about this topic changed?

Commit to Prayer

- If you have been seeking God for deliverance from the "giants" in your life, this week ask the Lord to reveal to you the one giant that He wants you to destroy in this next season of your life. You may even consider fasting for your spiritual breakthrough. If so, be led by the Holy Spirit as to the type of fast that He would require for your deliverance.
- Do a careful study of Deuteronomy 7. Ask the Holy Spirit to use this chapter to illuminate your mind and spirit to the process of deliverance and to show you what He requires of you as you participate in the process.
- Worship the Lord for being a strong Deliverer. Thank Him for knowing just how much you can bear in the process. Thank Him for His gentle and deliberate handling of you. Our God is a loving and tender God, and will not put more on us than we can bear, but He is ultimately committed to our total deliverance, and will do what He must to set our captive minds free.

Chapter 21

<u>Delivered From Shame</u>

"Instead of their shame my people will receive a double portion, and instead of disgrace they will rejoice in their inheritance."

Isa. 61:7

Chapter Theme

- Shame is a powerful stronghold that strips us of our value and worth. It leaves us feeling tarnished and stripped of our God-given glory. If God created us in His image, surely we are glorious beings, but one who has been shamed no longer radiates glory.

From the depths of His love for us, Jesus hung on the cross in great shame and dishonor, and in so doing, He not only has been eternally glorified by the Father, but He has also won back our glory for us. He promises to give us a double portion for our shame, and rejoicing for our disgrace as He faithfully rebuilds our gates.

Who's Guarding the Gates? Study Guide

Delivered From Shame

Questions for Discussion

1. According to John Milton – "Where there is shame, _____ _____ _____ _____."

2. Complete the sentence:
   God is resourceful and creative. As He undertakes the great and wonderful task of restoring our broken places, in this case, restoring the gate to the mind, He will use various scenarios, employing _____, and the like, as irritants, meant to flush out evil.

3. In your own words, what does Watchman Nee mean when he says that "everything is measured by God for us"?

4. Circle one: True or False
   Humility and shame are really one and the same.

5. How is "shame" defined in the dictionary?

6. You will often find that a person who has been shamed, but who sincerely desires to walk in the will of the Lord, will do public ministry with great fear, but _____ _____ _____ _____.

7. As Jesus Christ hung on the cross, He bore our _____ and _____ _____.

8. What does Hebrews 12:2 say?

9. Fill in the blanks:

   In humbling us, or in His exhortations to us to humble ourselves, it is never the will of God to destroy us. It is solely _____ _____ to His touch that comes to break the back of pride, selfishness, and rebellion in our lives, that causes us to *self*-destruct.

10. What does humility look like when God is administering it in our lives?

11. How have we benefited from Jesus' willingness to humble Himself, even at the expense of great shame?

12. The Lord allows us to work out our salvation with fear and trembling with humility, not under the _____ of _____ _____ _____.

13. What is the promise to us from God found in Isaiah 54:11-14?

14. What is the eighteenth building material needed in the reconstruction of our gates?

Conclusion

The giants of *Shame* and *Fear* will keep us in hiding the whole of our lives if we do not wholeheartedly seek God for deliverance. The Devil will keep us on lockdown behind his gates if we sheepishly allow him to. It must become our earnest desire to want to fulfill our destiny in Christ and to thoroughly finish the tasks that God predestined us to do when He allowed us to issue forth from our mothers' wombs. If we are willing and ready, God will work a mighty deliverance in our lives. He will give us a double portion of strength and anointing to boldly, victoriously walk in our calling, and bring great glory and honor to His name.

Applying God's Principles in our Daily Lives

Points to Ponder

- Are you cowering behind the giants of Shame and Fear, allowing them to dictate your every move and redefine your destiny? Knowing that it is not the will of God for His children to be crushed and diminished by shame, what will be your next move to break free from behind the Enemy's gates?
- Many times we blame others for our pain when it is really the sovereign hand of God exercising His creativity to bring about deliverance in our lives. Can you think of a time when you missed an opportunity for deliverance because you failed to recognize it as God working on your behalf? How can you better position yourself to realize when God is working in your life to refine you?
- God handed the giant, Goliath, over to David, who picked up five stones, ran toward Goliath, and slew him with one stone to the forehead. God is requiring us to deal aggressively with our giants, as well. His promise is to hand them over to us, just as He did for David. Do you have a giant standing right in front of you, daring you to deal with him, daring you to kill him? Are you ready to do exactly what God told you to do to destroy this giant?

Commit to Prayer

- Begin your devotion time this week by thanking the Lord for His promise to deliver you, and for His passionate commitment to perfecting all that concerns you.
- Ask the Lord to forgive you for not dealing aggressively with the giants in your life. Make a commitment to God and to yourself to completely destroy, one by one, every giant that God drives out before you.
- Joyfully receive God's grace and promise for a double portion for your shame, and rejoicing, as an inheritance for disgrace. (See Isa. 61:7)

Chapter 22

Where Are You Headed?
(Dealing With the Wall)

"Now the Angel of the Lord found her by a spring of water in the wilderness, by a spring on the way to Shur, and He said, "Hagar, Sarai's maid, where have you come from, and where are you going?" Gen. 16:7-8 (NKJV)

Chapter Theme

- There is a mile marker along our earthly pilgrimage beyond which it is dangerous for us to travel; that point is known as *the wall*. It is at the wall where God deals with the character flaws in us. He knows that unless those flaws are exposed and corrected, we will end up in a purposeless wilderness, trapped and imprisoned by character flaws, and ultimately, we will die in that wilderness. God's inspection of our fruit at the wall will afford us the opportunity to make necessary changes and adjustments to our character that will be to our benefit and for His glory.

Where Are You Headed?
(Dealing with the Wall)

Questions for Discussion

1. One cannot know where he is headed until he knows _____ _____ _____ _____ _____ .

2. What is the Hebrew definition of the word *Shur*?

3. What important question did the Angel of the Lord ask Hagar at the spring of water, and what was the significance of that question?

4. Complete the sentence:
   Without a renewed mind we will find ourselves _____ .
   _____ .

5. What was Hagar's response to the Angel's question to her? What does her response reveal about her sense of self-worth?

6. What was Balaam's character flaw?

7. Circle one:

   When we run into the wall along our journey and can go no further, we get frustrated and lash out at:

   a) the dog

   b) the cat

   c) our parents

   d) our second grade math teacher

   e) our ex

   f) the children

   g) the boss

   h) the pastor

   i) all of the above

8. What is the two-fold reason for the structured delay in our journey?

9. What will be the results if God allows us to continue along our journeys without having to stop at the wall?

10. According to Henri Nouwen, "_____ is the impulsive response to the experience of being _____."

11. What does the author say was primarily what set her free from the spirit of rage that controlled her life?

Where Are You Headed? (Dealing With the Wall)

12. What is the nineteenth building material for our gates?

13. What is the twentieth building material used in the reconstruction of our gates?

14. Why does the Holy Spirit meet us at the wall?

15. Complete the sentence:

    At the wall, He will call us to stand in the midst of His flames as He burns everything off of us that _____ _____. He will polish us up and finish us off just like silver is refined in the crucible, and like gold is tried in the fire.

16. What is the Hebrew definition of Hagar's name?

17. What did the Angel of the Lord command Hagar to do, and how did this command address her character flaw?

18. What do you believe is the significance of Hagar's response to the Angel's command?

19. What encouragement do we receive from John 17:4?

Who's Guarding the Gates? Study Guide

20. Complete the sentence:

    Every time we move in the direction of radical obedience to our God, _____ .

21. According to 2 Kings 13:18-19, why was Jehoash not able to completely defeat Aram?

22. Circle one: True or False

    Where you see mention in the Old Testament of a wall or gate being torn down by an enemy, it was a sure indication that a people had been disgraced.

23. Complete the sentence:

    However we came to be in the position of being exposed to repeated Enemy invasion, it is the Lord's pleasure to show us love and mercy, just as He did for Hagar, and to _____ and _____ our gates.

24. What was the outcome of David's pursuit of the Amalekites?

25. What does Revelation 21:2-4 promise us once we are safe inside Abba's gates?

26. What is the twenty-first building material needed in the reconstruction of our gates?

Conclusion

Living without walls and without the protection of our gates has changed who we are. We have all but forgotten who God has created us to be. Without the protection of our gates, we have been subjected to enemy invasion and enemy influences. We have allowed our Adversary to warp our Christian values and pervert our character. The path that we are headed down will only lead us to our destruction unless we make that pit stop at the wall and allow the Lord to point out and pluck off our sour fruits.

Our Lord reveals Himself to us in a fresh, new way when we stop and wait for His visitation upon us at the wall. It is there that He challenges us to conduct our own inspection as well. There, at the wall, He helps us to see ourselves as He sees us, past, present, and future. He destroys the lies that Satan has fed us about our identity, our position, our destiny, and our authority in Christ. He puts the pointed questions to us: *Where have you come from? Where are you now? Where are you trying to go?* As we answer those questions, with His help, we regain our perspective and we can rebuild our gates and get back on the right track as we wholeheartedly follow our Lord's wise instructions.

Applying God's Principles in Our Daily Lives

Points to Ponder

- The trials of life can weigh us down so heavily that we can easily lose our way and lose sight of our purpose in God. If we do not stay close to Jesus, we may never find our way back to the right path. Can you think of just such a time in your life when you lost your perspective, forgot who you were and had no sense of the purpose of God for your life? How did the Lord help you get back on course?
- God sends His Word into our lives to set us free from strongholds that come to defeat us. Have you experienced the power of His Word in your life breaking longstanding strongholds off of your mind? How did it happen? What was the process that you underwent before you could finally say that you were free?
- In this chapter, we learned that the Hebrew definition of Hagar's name is *flight*. For so long, Hagar allowed her name to define her character. Can you see yourself in Hagar? In what way(s)? What are you willing to do to change your character?

Where Are You Headed? (Dealing With the Wall)

Commit to Prayer

- If you are currently "on the run," in a dry place, lost, without a sense of purpose and without a sense of who you are anymore, challenge yourself to stop and ask the Lord to minister to your spirit. Seek the Lord in your dry place. Ask Him to restore your sense of purpose. Ask Him to break the strongholds of oppression off of your mind so that you can reclaim your identity in Him.
- If the damage to the gates to your mind has resulted in character flaws for you, confess those flaws by name. Repent of the things that you have done that you know are out of character for you as a child of God. Ask the Lord to help you to correct those flaws before you try to continue any further along your journey.
- If you have ever stopped short of giving God complete obedience, as we read Jehosah did in 2 Kings 13-18-19, confess your disobedience. Ask the Lord to forgive you and cleanse you from halfhearted obedience. Make up your mind to give the Lord one hundred percent obedience the next time He instructs you to do something.

Answer Key

Chapter 1

The Significance of the Gates

1. Abraham displayed this unusual obedience when he took his only son to the region of Moriah to offer him up to the Lord as a burnt sacrifice at the commandment of God (vv. 1-14).
2. Abraham never once argued with God concerning His unusual request. Instead, he chose to give God radical obedience.
3. It was through his obedience that the promise of Genesis 22:15-18 has been secured for us. ". . .and your descendants shall possess the gate of their enemies. In your seed all the nations of the earth shall be blessed, because you have obeyed My voice."
4. The Hebrew word for "possess" is *yaresh* (yaw-raysh'). It means: to occupy (by driving out previous tenants and possessing in their place); to seize, to rob, inherit, expel, impov-

erish, to ruin, cast out, disinherit, dispossess, to make poor, succeed.

5. (noun) - a beginning, an entrance or a mouth.

   (verb) - a stronghold, a fortress, a prison, or a hedge.

6. When we consider the definition of the word "gate" from a spiritual perspective, it doesn't take very much to see that the gates of our Adversary, the Devil, are designed to set up inescapable strongholds, fortresses and prisons in our lives.

7. thief, liar, rob, kill and destroy (John 10:10).

8. "I tell you the truth, I am the gate for the sheep. . .whoever enters through me will be saved."

9. However, because the people of God have failed to *guard the gates* to the Kingdom of God, we have become, as Isaiah 42:22 says, "...a people plundered and looted, all of them trapped in pits or hidden away in prisons. They have become plunder with no one to rescue them."

10. A journey through the Old Testament reveals to us that the gates were positioned at the entrances to the cities. They were considered places for city officials to discuss current events, and to transact business.

11. **Legal business** was handled at the gates. (Ruth 4:1-11)

    Criminal cases were solved at the gates. (Deut. 25:7-9)

    Proclamations were made at the gates. (Jer. 17:19-20)

    Festivities took place at the gates. (Ps. 24:7)

Answer Key

Political strategies were orchestrated at the gates to the cities. (2 Sam. 15:1-6)

12. **Places of authority** where one could both see and be seen. (Gen. 19:1-2; Judg. 18:14-17)

    These gates are also figurative for **satanic power**. (Matt. 16:18)

    They are figurative for **death**. (Is. 38:10)

    They are figurative for **righteousness**. (Ps. 118:19)

    They are figurative for **salvation**. (Matt. 7:14)

    They are figurative for **Heaven**. (Rev. 21:25)

13. Wood - These gates were easily burned down with fire, flimsy gates, gates erected with absolutely no constitution behind them; Bronze - Designed to keep the people of God imprisoned; Iron - Designed to keep God's people from receiving His divine provision; Precious Stones - These are the gates to the Holy City, Jerusalem, and they are God's gates. God's gates are durable and they cannot be destroyed!

14. humility

15. They complained against both God and Moses in saying, "We were better off in Egypt! Why did we ever leave Egypt?"

16. He feeds us occasional delicacies in the land of our captivity to numb us to the fact that we are indeed in prison.

17. We are "a chosen people, a royal priesthood, a holy nation, a people belonging to God, that you may declare the praises of him who called you out of darkness into his wonderful light."

18. Set a trap that they will like. Just before feeding time, you put a small amount of some kind of food that they will be attracted to just on the outside of the trap door, and put the bulk of the food just inside the trap door. The rodent will smell the food and walk right up to the trap and begin eating the lure, or the small amount of food on the outside of the trap door. Once the lure has done its job of drawing the animal to the trap and whetting its appetite, then the smell of the larger portion of food will call it all the way inside of the cage, and the mission has been accomplished. Satan lures us in the exact same way. When our flesh begins to crave the delicacies of sin, the devil understands that it's feeding time. He will design a lure of something tailor-made for us, something really sticky that we will not be able to break free from easily once we have had a taste. His lure will draw us and hold us in bondage behind his gates for years and years because he will see to it that we always have easy access to the larger portions of sin. Through our own lustful desires we are held captive behind the Enemy's gates.
19. We shut our heart gate to God by hardening our hearts. We shut off our ear gates to God by either pretending that we do not hear His instruction, or when we do hear Him, we make the choice to ignore Him. We shut off our mind gate by insisting on having our own way and resisting the mind of Christ.
20. Answers may vary.
21. The eyes, ears, mouth, heart, and mind.

22. His commandments were not too difficult, not out of their reach, but, He said, "The Word is very near you; it is in your mouth, and in your heart, so that you can obey it."
23. radical obedience

Chapter 2

Unclogging the Gates

1. Answers may vary.
2. Answers may vary.
3. Answers may vary.
4. Answers may vary.
5. false
6. We increase Satan's reign of authority at our ear gates.
7. fantasy
8. In the world of fantasy any and everything can happen. It is a world that the Devil has created for our sensual pleasure. In it we can have the ideal, perfect man or woman. Fantasy allows us to be in a relationship with a married man and suffer no consequences. It fools us into believing that we can have such torrid, forbidden relationships and that no one will ever discover our little secret. Fantasy has us believing that if one man doesn't work out, we can have another one better than him in a minute. The world of fantasy is also dangerous, because it will take us down a dark path chanting to ourselves the lie that if the man that we love walks out on us, we will never breathe again. The world of fantasy that revolves around secular music will keep us tied to a daydream, to a castle in the sky that will ultimately crash down upon us.
9. in the process of turning away from God.

Answer Key

10. by thinking they don't have any.
11. Answers may vary.
12. possesses the authority!
13. "to move in self-defense, to resist, to screen, to shield, to beat off, to resist invasion, to show fight, to stand one's ground, to stand in the gap."
14. trample our gates and to wreak havoc on our land, stealing, killing and destroying whatever he sees uncovered, unlocked, and unguarded.
15. eye gates, ear gates.
16. it is the devil in disguise.
17. "We perish by permitted things."

Chapter 3

When Reason is Asleep

1. conceived, birth, sin; sin, birth, death
2. (Answers will vary somewhat) Romanticism emerged from a desire for freedom, politically, and also freedom of thought, feeling, action, worship, and of tastes, as well as all the other freedoms. Romantics asserted that freedom is the right and property of one and all, though for each individual the kind and degree of freedom might vary. Those who affiliated themselves with Romanticism believed that the path to freedom was through imagination rather than reason, and functioned through

feeling rather than through thinking. For people living in the eighteenth century, the Middle Ages were the "dark ages," a time of barbarism, superstition, dark mystery, and miracle. The Romantic imagination stretched its perceptions of the Middle Ages into all the worlds of fantasy open to it, including the ghoulish, the infernal, the terrible, the nightmarish, the grotesque, the sadistic, and all the imagery that comes from the chamber of horrors when reason is asleep.

3. When *reason* is asleep, the creature begins to think that it knows better than its Creator. Thus, the lust for more knowledge, this unholy desire to feel something, anything, deeper and greater; the imaginations that lead us to think that we can be more than what God created us to be, even like God, is antagonistic towards God. This evil craving to know more than God knew we were able to handle in our finite state, causes us to seek to establish another kind of order; that order would otherwise be known as *disorder*; The thirst for more knowledge becomes evil when that which is given to us to know by God is simply not enough for us and we begin to try to uncover what He has hidden from us by some other means.

4. When we feel forgotten, slighted, or abandoned by God we will try to wrestle the answers out of His hands by consulting witches and warlocks. We use tarot cards and 8-balls, attend séances, go to palm readers, consult mediums and fortune tellers, read our astrological forecasts.

Answer Key

5. Answers may vary.

6. She had set her heart on pilgrimage without the Shepherd, convinced that she knew what was best *for her l*ife and how to achieve those goals a lot faster without His assistance. A pilgrimage without the Shepherd is a hike into the chambers of Hell itself.

Chapter 4

Do You Wish To See?

1. 70%

2. the eye

3. lamp, body; full, light; full, darkness. (Matthew 6:22-23)

4. "all the eye does is gather light."

5. while the eye sees the illusion, the brain is remembering the image as recorded prior to the illusion.

6. We know what we know about Him, but when our lives fall prey to the ravaging effects of sin, and we find ourselves held fast in the grip of pain, we begin to formulate a false impression about God. It is then that we mold a god with our own hands. We come to the conclusion that God is cold, sadistic, and merciless. We reason that since He is not answering us, or coming to our rescue, then either He cannot hear, or He is as powerless as we are.

7. blindness, justification; (Answers will vary slightly as students expound on the scripture in their own words). "This is the judgment, that the Light has come into the world, and men loved the darkness rather than the Light, for their deeds were evil. For everyone who does evil hates the Light, and does not come to the Light for fear that his deeds will be exposed. But he who practices the truth comes to the Light, so that his deeds may be manifested as having been wrought in God." John 3:19-21 (NASB)
8. "Do you wish to get well?"
9. "Lord, we want our eyes to be opened!"
10. false
11. no match; spiritual arsenal
12. release mighty divine power
13. God will be "a source of strength to those who turn back the battle at the gate."
14. true
15. The optical illusion that Satan created presented the forbidden fruit as a source of greater power, or a greater light, a deeper realm of knowledge than that which God, her Creator had made available to her. They would become gods in their own rights, was the message that Satan was trying to communicate to both Adam and Eve.
16. e) all of the above

Answer Key

17. This enticing spirit makes a happily married man look outside of his marriage for something more, something different. This spirit causes a perfectly healthy young woman to starve herself to death to conform to an unappeasable, distorted and unrealistic media image of the perfect woman. This monster called "the media" has been given the power to dictate to her who and what she "should" look like to be considered acceptable by the world's standards. To a single person, watching all of his/her friends get married, this spirit plants a seed in their minds that manifests as the thought that God is withholding their "good thing" from them. To the little-known pastor who has been entrusted with fifty congregants, seeing mega-churches on The Word Network and TBN causes him to feel dissatisfied with the few sheep that God has entrusted to his care.
18. position, authority
19. discernment

Chapter 5

A Holy Gaze

1. She had been gazing at the world so intently for so long that she knew only how to adorn herself as the world's images adorned themselves.
2. begin, reflect

3. Students may choose from any of the statistics on pornography noted in this chapter.
4. the veil is removed, and we, then, "with unveiled faces are reflecting the Lord's glory, and are being transformed into His likeness with ever increasing (not decreasing) glory, which comes from the Lord, who is the Spirit."
5. Jesus had full control of His eye gates. He loved the Father more; thoroughly understood His mission, and was radical in His obedience.
6. valuable clues from Him that will shape our lives
7. holiness
8. Sometimes we have to work at seeing clearly. Sometimes we need the Holy Spirit to bring truth to us in stages in much the same way as a camera allows us to see objects clearly that are far away as we turn the lens to bring them sharply into focus. Sometimes we need our lenses cleaned to see clearly. And always, we need the Savior's touch upon our eyes so that when we look at men, we see men as men, and not as trees.
9. e) all of the above
10. what we think we see
11. It is so important for us to take what we see with our natural eyes into the light of God's presence. Sitting in His presence we wait, we listen, we hear, and there we receive council from the Spirit of the Lord God in discerning with the spiritual eye what He has allowed us to see with the natural eye.

Answer Key

12. This means that we must choose to *sit* and *wait* for Him to speak to us. We must wait for a holy unction from Him, an unmistakable movement upon our hearts, a sensing of His presence in the place of prayer, and that His presence has left a deposit upon our spirits. Standing in the Lord's council, we sense His heart, receive His mind, and hear His voice over every other voice.

13. "I tell you the truth, the Son can do nothing by himself; he can only do what he sees his Father doing, because whatever the Father does, the Son also does."

14. It was important to Jesus to leave us an example, a method, if you will, of judging matters and for coming to righteous conclusions. His example cautions us not to make hasty decisions based exclusively upon what we see and certainly not based upon what we project from the inside out. Our Lord is righteous in all of His ways. Lest we be tempted to judge a matter solely based upon what we see, God has given us a standard to follow and uphold. We allow so much impurity to flood our eye gates that we must be ever conscious to keep looking to Jesus. We must keep returning to the true standard and keep giving Him permission to tear down our faulty gates and to rebuild our gates in righteousness.

15. to gaze with wide-open eyes, as at something remarkable; to discern clearly, to behold, perceive and to take heed.

16. faith

Chapter 6

A Faulty Lamp

1. ultimately cause our lamps to go completely out.
2. useless, compromise
3. Moses, Elijah, Jeremiah, Isaiah, Ezekiel, Micaiah, Samuel, Jesus, the Christ; prophets
4. "The fear of man will prove to be a snare."
5. monetary gain
6. Answers may vary.
7. a bowl of stew
8. Students may answer by citing any one of the statistics given in this chapter.
9. crimes of passion, crimes committed by Satan and his posse of demons; stealing, killing, destroying
10. Because in the midst of years and years of discouragement, sorrow, disappointment, shame and deep grief, she kept her composure. In the midst of Peninnah's evil assaults upon her to provoke her to jealousy, though Hannah wept bitterly, she maintained her focus on the God who was able to avenge her.
11. an intense and purposeful gaze; no less loved by God
12. fear
13. rebellion, disobedience
14. jealously eyed

Answer Key

15. Our pride will not accept the fact that someone else can be as gifted or more gifted than ourselves. We will begin to look at them with eyes of suspicion, wondering where they are, what meetings they are attending that we were not asked to attend, who they are hanging out with, what they are being asked to do in the church that we have not been asked to do. We will find ourselves being unloving towards them and refusing to encourage them in their area of giftedness, especially if they are gifted in the same area in which we are gifted. We may even find ourselves trying to get them to leave the church, just so that we can rid our immediate environment of all potential rivals.

16. We must be very careful in our walk with God to make radical obedience a must. When God chooses to exalt us, we must humbly submit to His instructions, or else we can be sure that our replacement is on the way.

Chapter 7
Bring Him the Broken Pieces

1. false
2. the heartfelt, simple, yet desperate prayer, prayed in brokenness of spirit and lining up with the revealed will of God
3. "Keep, and guard your heart with all vigilance, and above all that you guard, for out of it flow the springs [issues] of life"
4. "boundaries," or "borders"

5. honor, love, courage, integrity
6. it meant certain death.
7. sovereign
8. Had he been able to grab hold of the grace of God made available to him, that grace would have carried him through the trial to a victorious end. That grace would have given him a peace that would have surpassed any lack of understanding with which he had been wrestling. That grace would have washed over his heart and washed out any bitterness, preventing any bitter roots from being established there.
9. entitled
10. c) 80%
11. Per the author: I failed, as a parent, to guard the gates of my children's hearts when I rebelliously married a man who was an agnostic some 29 years ago. A few years into the marriage, he fathered my daughter, and four years later, he was gone, leaving the heart of a once-confident little girl, who was convinced that she was the apple of her daddy's eyes, completely shattered. With my own hands, I helped to tear her gates down before I could ever help her build strong ones.
12. trust

Chapter 8

A Holy House

1. Answers may vary.
2. a) Outer – body; b) Holy Place – soul; c). Holy of Holies – spirit
3. f) all of the above
4. love us enough to chastise us, convict us, prune us, refine us, forgive us, wash us, heal us, sanctify us and glorify us.
5. "spirit, burning"
6. Answers may vary. Hebrews 10:19-22.
7. The heart that is perfect towards God is the heart that chooses to trust God without having yet laid hold of His promises, or having received the answers to the things that we have petitioned Him for, in the place of prayer. It is even the heart that is fearful, yet willing, willing to be made *quiet before God.* It is the heart of the child of God who is pressing on to God, perhaps making mistakes along the way, but getting up and getting back in the press towards God.
8. So often we miss His visitation either because of the noisiness that we allow to take over so much of our lives, or because we have not taken Him seriously.

Chapter 9

Let's Play Dress-Up!

1. the high price of following in His steps
2. brazen altar
3. death of something living
4. sacrificial, public death
5. by the manner in which we attend to our flesh. We treat it with collagen, Botox it, suck it out, slice it, lift it, nip it, and tuck it. We will buy a new suit, a new pair of shoes, a new dress, a new purse, or a new shade of lipstick every week. We color our hair so much that we cannot even remember what color God made it originally. We wear false eyelashes, and colored contacts, an assortment of wigs, and weaves—dreads today, and bald tomorrow!
6. Complete surrender and brokenness before God. The first step is to lay all of our heart on the altar – every broken, fractured, shattered, hardened, cold, grief-stricken or numb piece of it!
7. The human heart is easily deceived. Satan knows that, and so he uses those *things* as distractions to keep the people of God blinded and blissfully content right where they are, and inwardly, secretly afraid to venture past the superficiality of the Outer Court.
8. Answers may vary.

Answer Key

9. "I know your deeds, that you are neither cold nor hot. I wish you were either one or the other! So, because you are lukewarm — neither hot nor cold — I am about to spit you out of my mouth."

10. We must be willing to do the same for His sake, to ". . .offer our bodies as living sacrifices, holy and pleasing to God — this is your spiritual act of worship" (Romans 12:1).

11. He is our Helper. He anchors us in turbulent times so that we do not become completely unraveled at the seams, so that we do not cast away our confidence in Him. When we are weak, He makes us strong. When we are afraid, He gives us courage. He helps us to become more than what we are.

12. Isaiah 29:13.

13. Our hearts are clean and we are covered in Jesus' blood, clothed in His righteousness, consecrated and set apart for His service, and proud to be called by His name. We won't have to *play* dress-up. The fabric of our Christianity will be woven throughout our being, heart, mind, body and soul.

Chapter 10

Good Tree – Good Fruit! Bad Tree – Bad Fruit!

1. Answers may vary.
2. integrity
3. "Make a tree good, and its fruit will be good, or else make a tree bad and its fruit will be bad. For a tree is known by its fruit."

4. *who, what;* place, evolving
5. to endure, stay under, submit to the process
6. false
7. a stronger man
8. We extend our hands in an attempt to tend to the wounds of others, only to have the pus and poison and the stench of our own unattended wounds spill onto, and further infect the ones to whom we are attempting to administer healing.
9. quarantine
10. false
11. "Come out from among them, and be ye separate! Touch no unclean thing! Come out from it, and be ye pure."
12. The same thing that happens to rotten fruit; it stinks. It stinks of rebellion and disobedience and ultimately, it becomes the tragic stench of death!
13. Jesus' desire for us is that, as His children, we will bear fruit that remains, fruit that is useful and beneficial to someone else.
14. patience, hope

Chapter 11

Thy Will Be Done

1. false
2. willingness, readiness
3. Proverbs 14:12

Answer Key

4. to liberate us from the grip of Satan's lies
5. "God has bound all men over to disobedience so that He may have mercy on them all."
6. "even when the heart sustained serious injury, the mind still functioned."
7. When we depend entirely upon our mental coping skills to sustain us, and to deliver us in the wake of emotional trauma, all we do is open up the gates to our minds to unwittingly allow Satan to begin establishing powerful strongholds that will then take us years to tear down.
8. "Put no confidence in the flesh."
9. When we fail to present our damaged hearts to the Lord for cleansing and for healing, then the calcification process begins. Those areas surrounding our hearts, once smooth and soft, once accepting, loving, merciful, and kind, now become hardened scar tissue, unloving, bitter, cold, and aloof. We find ourselves unable to empathize with the suffering of others, when in actuality, having suffered so much ourselves, we should be the very ones who have the ability to bear the compassion of Christ in the face of others' sufferings.
10. Jeremiah 7:23-24
11. "My Father. . .not as I will, but as you will."

Chapter 12

The Words We Speak

1. Answers may vary.
2. separated the issues
3. "Bless those who persecute you; bless and do not curse."
4. to go beyond that which can simply be accomplished by our flesh, to that which can only be accomplished by the help of the Holy Spirit residing within us.
5. "Without Me, you can do nothing."
6. false
7. "gaming ethics," bluffing," "artful negotiating."
8. Romans 1:18-30. Paul says that when we "suppress the truth by wickedness" we will experience the "wrath of God," and eventually, God will allow us to be "held captive to our own sinful ways," namely, "sexual immorality, wickedness, covetousness, maliciousness, envy, murder, strife and deceit," to name a few (vs. 29).
9. truth
10. "The wisdom of this world is foolishness in God's sight. As it is written; He catches the wise in their own craftiness."
11. To the degree that we are committed to abiding in the Word of God, to obeying His voice, to embracing His truth, to walking in truth and to telling the truth when our backs are up against the wall, we will be empowered though the Holy Spirit to declare

Answer Key

and decree God's truth over the lies sown by Satan, the father of all lies. We will be empowered not only to undo his evil works, but like our Big Brother in the faith, Jesus, the Christ, we will also be empowered to completely *abolish* his works, and take possession of his gates.
12. fortify our gates against deception and error.
13. "the gates of hell will not prevail against us"
14. mush mouths.
15. generations yet to come.
16. false; Isa. 20; Ezek. 4; Isa. 53; Matt. 27:41-44, or John 10:17-18 (Any one of these scriptures are acceptable answers).
17. Answers may vary.
18. truth

Chapter 13

Bent by A Word

1. can be a life sentence.
2. Adam names his firstborn son Cain, which means, "to provoke to jealousy, chant, or wail at a funeral, lament, and mourning mother." His second son he names Abel, which means, "emptiness, vanity, transitory and unsatisfactory.
3. As were their names, so were their lives. Abel, murdered by his brother Cain, and Cain, destined to be a drifter, a restless

wanderer over the face of the earth; a man for whom the ground would no longer yield its crops.

4. When a mother calls her child "stupid," "lazy," or "good for nothing," she bends that child's spirit, and makes her an emotional and a mental cripple.

5. He had to purify him.

6. Answers will vary somewhat.

7. "Whoever spreads slander is a fool."

8. "Lord, who may dwell in your sanctuary? Who may live on your holy hill? He whose walk is blameless, and who does what is righteous, who speaks the truth from his heart, and has no slander on his tongue, who does his neighbor no wrong, and casts no slur on his fellowman ... He who does these things will never be shaken."

9. Our discouragement will fade away; we will rise up out of a place of despair; The Word of God will elevate us up and out of depression; God's spoken Word will break strongholds of defeat off of our lives; we will gain new hope, and our hope will convert to joy, and our joy will result in even more worship of the One, and Only, True and Living God; Satan's power will be greatly diminished, and he will be sorely humiliated, and we, the saints of the Most High God, will experience a foretaste of glory divine.

10. "But I say to you that men will have to give account on the Day of Judgment for every careless word that they have spoken. For

Answer Key

by your words you will be acquitted, and by your words you will be condemned."

11. . . .there are rules that require our obedience if we are to take possession of the gates of our enemies.

12. She began wearing full makeup every day of her life for the next thirty-seven years. Linda would remain in this bondage to cosmetics, and the superficial need to "keep up appearances," for the next thirty-seven years. She also lost her true identity behind the mask of cosmetics that she donned every day. Her belief in her father's spoken words caused her to get stuck on concentrating only on trying to look pretty for thirty-seven years. She was unable to see that she was more than just a "pretty face."

13. false.

14. Proverbs 3:27 exhorts us with these words, "Do not withhold good from those who deserve it, when it is in your power to act." Romans 15:1-3, "We who are strong ought to bear the failings of the weak and not to please ourselves. Each of us should please his neighbor for his good, to build him up. For even Christ did not please himself."

15. Because of his expression of gratitude, Jesus made him *completely* whole.

16. ". . .you will ask what you desire, and it shall be done for you."

17. wisdom

Chapter 14
Choose Your Battles

1. Answers may vary.
2. If we can see ourselves as the warriors that we are, then we will prepare ourselves to do battle as warriors. We will be more likely to respond to the snares of Satan as a warrior would respond, with a well thought out strategy to avoid the pitfalls and to destroy our enemy, and not merely as a naïve Christian who is completely caught off guard by Satan's traps.
3. As opposed to firing off back at the offender in kind, repaying offense for offense, as an enlightened warrior, we can instead approach our offender quickly, in the spirit of love and reconciliation, to let them know how what they have done has caused us to feel hurt.
4. Answers may vary.
5. Jesus said, in Matthew 18:21-22 that there is to be no limit on the number of times that we extend forgiveness to an offender.
6. It lets us know that "Our struggle is *not* against flesh and blood, but against the rulers, against the authorities, against the powers of this dark world, and against the spiritual forces of evil in the heavenly realms."
7. false
8. All Jehoshaphat and the army of Judah were instructed by God to do was to march out onto the battlefield and face the enemy,

Answer Key

sing songs and give thanks to God. God said that is all you have to do, just "face the enemy," and I will do all the fighting for you; God caused the armies that had come out against Judah to turn on themselves and they effectively slaughtered each other. The army of Judah was completely unharmed in that battle.

9. "Stick to the path; stick to the path. This is not your fight."
10. "From such people - turn away. . .they will grow worse and worse. . .but you must continue in the things which you have learned and been assured of, knowing from whom you have learned them" (2 Tim. 3:5, 13 and 14).
11. "I will contend with those who contend with you, and your children I will save. I will make your oppressors eat their own flesh; and they will be drunk with their own blood, as with wine. Then all mankind will know that I, the Lord, am your Savior, your Redeemer, the Mighty One of Jacob.
12. faithfulness

Chapter 15

Abiding in Jesus – The Discipline of Waiting

1. meno (men'-o), to stay in a given place, state or expectancy; to continue, dwell, be present, endure, remain, and to stand.
2. Jesus said in John 15:7, "If you abide in Me and My words abide in you, you will ask what you desire and it will be done for you." He was giving us a conditional promise. This kind of

abiding requires discipline. For the twenty-first century saint, this presents a unique challenge because we live in a society where we must have everything at our fingertips, right now! The virtue of patience, developed from having to wait, has become such an underdeveloped fruit of the Spirit, and the dangerous, subtle, but not so subtle message that we are being fed is that *waiting* is *not* a good thing.

3. "watch, pray" (Matt. 26:41)
4. Answers may vary.
5. to calm down, to stop working in overdrive, to quiet itself, to hold its peace and to be *astonished* at its God.
6. that the Holy Spirit would stir up within us the gift of "hunger for Jesus."
7. "But the people who know their God shall prove themselves strong, and shall stand firm, and do great exploits for God."
8. the trustworthy servant who busied himself with the tasks left to his care in his master's absence
9. We must commit ourselves to devote much time to reading and studying, meditating on and saturating our souls with God's Word, worship, praise and prayer as we wait before Him.
10. false
11. truth, truth
12. One of the tools that Satan has been using to soften the blow of his coming deceptions is reality TV. This tool of deception has the world captivated!

Answer Key

13. "Then you will know the truth, and the truth will set you free." (John 8:32); "When the Spirit of truth comes, He will guide you into all truth" (John 16:13); And again, He tells us that "We will know the Spirit of truth because He dwells with us, and in us" (John 14:17).
14. poor stewards
15. false
16. a worthy man, woman, boy or girl among them who would build up the wall, and stand in the gap before Me on behalf of the land, that I should not destroy it;
17. none
18. It is by actively waiting in His presence.
19. discipline of abiding

Chapter 16
Are You Ready to Rumble?

1. Answers may vary.
2. slumber
3. busy, commissioned us to do
4. "Without me you can do nothing." Answers to second part of this question may vary.
5. Students may choose from any one of the scenarios discussed in this section of the chapter, or they may personalize their answers.

6. False
7. The stench of death is in our homes — the institution of marriage is dying; Death has boldly stormed the gates of our schools, literally! Our children are murdering each other in the classrooms and the hallways of higher learning. The stench of death is in our streets. Violence on our streets has reached astounding proportions. We are horrified as we watch the cold brazenness of children stomping and beating each other to death in broad daylight and then cold-heartedly blasting a video of the beating on YouTube! The stench of death is in our churches. Pastors, clergy and licensed ministers try to minister to the broken, the bruised, the demonically oppressed and the afflicted, but they are unable to meet their needs because they are operating in the flesh, full up of flesh and lacking anointing.
8. "The Spirit gives life; the flesh profits nothing."
9. *gregoreuo* - literally means to "keep awake, or to be vigilant; *egeiro*, which means to rouse (lit. from sleep, from sitting or lying. . .; or fig. . . .from inactivity. . .):. . .to stand."
10. g) all of the above
11. weak, unprepared, fight
12. There is nothing wrong with those prayers, but they are *other* people's prayers. They are not *your* prayers to God. If we can plop in a CD, and just listen to someone else praying, while all we do is close our eyes, and say, "Amen," this does nothing but make us more comatose, and lazy.

Answer Key

13. "In the morning, O' Lord, you will hear *my* voice" (Ps. 5:3), and "In the morning *my prayer* comes before You" (Ps. 88:13). "Let the words of *my mouth*, and the meditation of *my heart* be acceptable unto You" (Ps.19:14).
14. punch is in the Word of God!
15. the devil never saw coming!
16. no longer even expecting God to answer our prayers, and quite frankly, we wonder if He is even listening.
17. We can have confidence in prayer, when praying the will of God; that He will hear us and answer us. We can step in the ring expecting to conquer!
18. sanctified
19. sanctification

Chapter 17
Which Way Did I Go?

1. operating as double-minded individuals
2. Answers may vary.
3. where we experienced the loss
4. ". . .a double-minded man is unstable in all he does."
5. "Double-minded" is translated in the Greek as *dipsuchos*. By definition, it means to be "two spirited."

6. to "heal the brokenhearted, to proclaim liberty to the captives and recovery of sight to the blind, to set at liberty those who are bruised."
7. *thrauo,* (*throw'-o*), which means to crush; *agnumi* which is to "break", "wreck" or "crack",. . .to sunder (by separation of the parts;. . .a shattering to minute fragments);. . . to disrupt."
8. Satan's goal in the bruising is that we be completely shattered, cracked asunder. But the goal of God is that our brokenness will lead us back to Him, and make us more useful to Him. (Rom. 8:28)
9. We must bear this in mind as we interface with unbelievers and as we co-exist and co-labor with our brothers and sisters in Christ—that we are not seeing the whole picture, only a fragment of the person God created them to be. With this understanding, we should be more willing to extend compassion, mercy and love towards each other, and too, because most of us have sorely neglected our own mental and emotional health, we are often functioning out of our fragmentation.
10. fragmentation, inconsistent, restless, disorderly.
11. d) all of the above.
12. to destroy the works of the Devil
13. d) all of the above
14. stability
15. false
16. "For I am the Lord who heals you."

Answer Key

17. biological; psychological; environmental/sociological
18. They were not made completely whole.
19. to save. . .to deliver, or protect
20. false
21. the Devil comes back to bother us again!
22. Here we see an enemy scheming to invade a people who have just recovered from an assault and have begun to settle down in peace. While they are trying to put their lives back together again, the enemy plots to catch them off guard, "a peaceful and an unsuspecting people – all of them living without walls and without gates and bars.
23. Answers will vary somewhat. Adult survivors of childhood trauma may very well have survived their unique awful childhood experiences, but they are now, as adults, mentally, spiritually, emotionally, and even physically, in great trouble and much disgrace. Finding themselves "back in the province" so to speak, in situations where they have to submit to a cruel supervisor, or in a marriage with an abusive spouse, or trying to raise a troubled teen who is strung out on drugs, they soon discover themselves to be emotionally handicapped. They are disgraced by having to repeat history because they have not sought a cure for their soul's *diseases*. They are disgraced by the sheer haunting memories, and ill-timed, triggered flashbacks of yesterday's shameful abuses. They are in trouble and disgraced because their own traumatic childhood experiences, having

gone unattended, have rendered them incapable of possessing the tools necessary to successfully resolve their all too strangely familiar present difficult life issues.

24. We choose not to deal with the unpleasant situation by creatively shutting it out. When a survivor of childhood trauma experiences a dark night of the soul, which threatens to take them back to some horrible memory, they simply close the shutters on the dark memory by using one of the following three coping mechanisms, *repression, denial, or dissociation.*

25. repression; denial; dissociation

26. False. Denial says, "This is not happening."

27. To stand in the gap you must be a whole individual. We cannot effectively intercede, pray, or stand in the gap for anything if:

- our perceptions on critical matters are distorted
- we are subconsciously trying to regain the control that was stolen from us, through abuse, while we were still a child
- our manner of processing things mentally has been severely altered from normal
- our past coping skills have taught us that it is necessary to *change the meaning of a thing* to make its existence more palatable
- if we are fragmented souls, having no sense of who we are, to position ourselves in such a highly charged spiritual atmosphere (standing in the gap), attempting to wage war against demonic principalities and powers of darkness is a dangerous thing.

28. 1 Corinthians 13:11

Answer Key

29. Adults must put away childish things and begin the hard process of working out their soul's salvation with much "fear and trembling" to face the challenges of adult life as healthy and whole beings.
30. courage

Chapter 18
A Candidate for Change

1. by knowing others
2. true
3. Psychologists will tell you that the emotion of fear causes the body to produce a rush of adrenaline that is meant to assist the one who is in danger to either run or to fight back. This is what is commonly known as the *flight or fight* syndrome.
4. The gates are open for this child to subconsciously, unknowingly house the spirits of anger and rage beginning from that very moment where the gates have been violated.
5. wheels, prophecy
6. "to shift, to mutate, a conversion (gradual change), revolution, metamorphosis, to turn the corner."
7. Things we could never accomplish in our old sinful, bound state, we can now accomplish in our transformed state, that is, in the Spirit's power. Places we could never go physically, spiritually, emotionally, and mentally, having been bound by the traumatic

experiences of our childhood, and controlled by our own irrational resolutions, we are now gradually freed to go as we walk in step with the Holy Spirit through a renewed mind, a mind that has undergone a radical conversion.

8. We can achieve a renewed mind as we are deliberate to make daily applications of the Word of God directly to the particular areas of struggle in our lives.
9. Many people with mental issues want to get better without having to do the required work to become whole.
10. Go face your pain!
11. in the journey
12. true
13. "He who conceals his sins does not prosper, but whoever confesses and renounces them, finds mercy."

Chapter 19

My Mind's Made Up

1. motherboard
2. They organize the brain by creating pathways that govern everything we do, from breathing and sleeping, to thinking and feeling.
3. false
4. the brain may discard them.

Answer Key

5. If we look at how the brain cells function and are formed, we see that in unhealthy relationships where the child is repeatedly neglected, rejected, and mistreated by the primary caregiver, the synapses for that type of unhealthy interaction are strengthened. Meanwhile, the synapses for healthy bonding are discarded, making it possible for the child to grow up and do pretty good at keeping those irrational, self-imprisoning resolutions that we discussed in previous chapters.
6. body will be allowed to go.
7. are all vain attempts
8. Zechariah 4:6 also tells us that anything that we are going to accomplish in this life that is going to be lasting and beneficial to us, to others and to the kingdom of God, must be accomplished by the Holy Spirit, not by force of will, or by our little, bitty, finite strength.
9. personal, spiritual, emotional, mental
10. It could very well be that God has called a timeout for the express purpose of giving them the opportunity to focus on becoming whole.
11. b) cuts it off
12. to restore our souls
13. restore and remake
14. By repeatedly showering us with His never-ending love, we will begin to believe that we are worthy of being loved, and accepted.
15. brokenness

Chapter 20

Looking Back

1. little by little
2. Answers may vary.
3. true
4. forgiveness
5. completely destroy them
6. process
7. Years of living in trauma have made them so accustomed to existing in shock mode that the mundane is not enough to satisfy their heightened senses. This is why many survivors of long-term trauma end up on drugs. They still need a high. This also accounts for the reason why some of the nicest people that you know always seem to never be content unless there is some kind of drama going on in their lives. No one in their right mind wants to stay in a toxic relationship, but for these, toxicity in relationships is familiar to them. It's all they know.
8. may find it extremely difficult to see any benefit in truth.
9. God's truth
10. Isaiah 28:14-18
11. God gave His only begotten Son for you and me and for all victims of injustice precisely because of His great love for us. Jesus willingly went to the cross and died for just such victims. In all His sufferings He has identified with the sufferings of every

victim of such heinous crimes committed against their personhood. The truth is that we live in a fallen world where people are greatly influenced by Satan and his demonic hosts. Injustices will occur on this earth daily, and who knows whose turn it will be to suffer next, but Jesus does stand in the midst of our sufferings with us. When we suffer abuses, humiliation, tortures and torment, our Savior's heart is greatly grieved. As He wept at the tomb of Lazarus (John 11:35), so He weeps over us, so great is His love for us. The Holy Spirit comforts us when it seems that no one else cares and we feel that we cannot be comforted, for He has said, "I will not leave you comfortless: I will come to you." (John 3:16, Is. 53, Heb. 4:14-16, Heb. 5:7-10).

12. holds us together

Chapter 21

Delivered From Shame

1. there is also fear."
2. co-workers, family members, supervisors, church leadership
3. Answers may vary.
4. false
5. "'to be stained or tarnished, and to have one's glory stripped away."
6. they will do it.
7. sin; our shame

8. "For the joy set before Him, He endured the cross, despising the shame."
9. our *resistance*
10. it embodies (not discounts) every aspect of who we are in Christ, including our uniqueness, our personhood, value, worth, and esteem.
11. He opened the gates to eternal life for us to enter.
12. bondages, shame and humiliation
13. "O afflicted city, lashed by storms and not comforted, I will build you with stones of turquoise, your foundations with sapphires. I will make your battlements of rubies, your gates of sparkling jewels, and all your walls of precious stones." This is God's promise to us, that out of the depths of His great love and concern for us, He will fortify us and strengthen us who have endured great trials. He will make our walls and gates strong and beautiful. He will reestablish us in "righteousness."
14. humility

Answer Key

Chapter 22

Where Are You Headed?
(Dealing With the Wall)

1. from whence he has come.
2. "...a wall..."
3. "Hagar, Sarai's maid, *where have you come from, and where are you going?*"; one cannot know where he is headed until he knows from whence he has come.
4. going through the motions of ministry, feeling nothing but claiming to be doing God's work.
5. *"I am...running away..."*; she doesn't even have a sense of who she is
6. he was a greedy man.
7. i) all of the above
8. One part is self-will; the other part is God's will.
9. either we will fall, hurting ourselves and others, and great will be that fall, or we will succeed in gaining the world, but losing our very souls.
10. anger; deprived
11. The Word of God
12. The Word of God
13. gentleness
14. to conduct an inspection of our fruit.
15. fails to pass His inspection.

16. flight
17. "Go back to your mistress and submit to her." The Lord challenged her to stop running and face herself.
18. Answers may vary.
19. God wants no less for each of us than that we fulfill our destinies in Him. It is in fulfilling our destinies that we bring Him the most glory.
20. We get to take possession of an enemy's gate.
21. God's instructions require our complete obedience if we desire to walk in the fullness of His plan for our lives. When we fall short of complete obedience, we subject ourselves to some very serious consequences, one of which is our own defeat.
22. true
23. repair; rebuild
24. "David recovered *everything* the Amalekites had taken, including his two wives. Nothing was missing: young or old, boy or girl, plunder or anything else they had taken. David brought everything back."
25. We will never experience shame, or fear, death, pain, or sorrow again. Once we are safe inside Abba's gates, our Heavenly Daddy will hold us in His loving arms and wipe away every tear from our eyes.
26. love

A TIMELY AND AMAZING
MUST **R**EAD

Who's Guarding the Gates?
Nancy L. Robinson

This powerful book will have you convinced that not everything that was lost, or stolen by the Enemy, is gone forever. By a divine strategy of radical obedience – you can recover all that God intends for you to recover.

Who's Guarding the Gates? Study Guide is really exceptional! Other study guides can feel like an afterthought, are disjointed from the book they accompany, or do not provide enough prodding for the readers' critical thinking. This guide stands apart in that the author's careful consideration shines through; it truly is a great addition for the book and adds another dimension of understanding rather than simply adding content.

The author carefully includes both discussion questions and summaries in this book. Together they really make the guide dynamic. Including the quotations at the beginning of each chapter section really communicate the underlying issue that the author seeks to address. It takes abstract concepts of morality/spirituality and makes them more concrete for the readers– by Vanessa Correa – Xulon Editor